The Effective Teacher's Guide to Dyslexia and Other Specific Learning Difficulties

Specific learning difficulties such as dyslexia, dyspraxia and dyscalculia can cause poor performance in school and may lead to emotional problems and low self-esteem. Children with such difficulties need a high level of understanding, encouragement and support from their teacher in order to achieve their full potential in an inclusive environment.

The Effective Teacher's Guide to Dyslexia and Other Specific Learning Difficulties offers the classroom teacher practical advice, information and enlightenment that will help them to bridge the gap between theory and practice, and equip them with a range of strategies with which to tackle everyday classroom situations. This book expertly guides the reader through:

◆ the legal and policy contexts;
◆ an explanation of terms and definitions;
◆ interventions and rationale;
◆ approaches related to different curriculum subjects.

Taking account of recent policy changes, and with an emphasis on what works in the classroom, this book will prove a practical, readable and invaluable resource for the busy practitioner.

Michael Farrell is an independent educational consultant and recognised expert in special education. He has written or edited over 30 acclaimed education books.

New Directions in Special Educational Needs

By focusing firmly on what really works in practice with children with special educational needs, this highly practical series will enlighten and inform any busy teacher eager to know more about individual difficulties, and who wants to make inclusion a reality for their pupils.

All books in the series concentrate on the educational implications of certain special educational needs. They also consider the legal obligations of schools, what teachers can do to support and encourage inclusive learning in their classroom, and where they can go for additional support and advice. Packed full of down-to-earth yet authoritative advice, this series will provide teachers with everything they need to ensure their pupils with special educational needs are effectively and properly supported.

Titles in the Series (all by Michael Farrell)

The Effective Teacher's Guide to Behavioural, Emotional and Social Difficulties
Practical strategies

The Effective Teacher's Guide to Autism and Communication Difficulties
Practical strategies

The Effective Teacher's Guide to Dyslexia and Other Specific Learning Difficulties
Practical strategies

The Effective Teacher's Guide to Moderate, Severe and Profound Learning Difficulties
Practical strategies

The Effective Teacher's Guide to Sensory Impairment and Physical Disability
Practical strategies

The Effective Teacher's Guide to Dyslexia and Other Specific Learning Difficulties

Practical strategies

Michael Farrell

Routledge
Taylor & Francis Group

LONDON AND NEW YORK

First published 2006
by Routledge
2 Park Square, Milton Park, Abingdon, Oxon OX14 4RN

Simultaneously published in the USA and Canada
by Routledge
270 Madison Ave, New York, NY 10016

Routledge is an imprint of the Taylor & Francis Group

Typeset in Times New Roman and Gill by
Florence Production Ltd, Stoodleigh, Devon
Printed and bound in Great Britain by
Bell & Bain Ltd, Glasgow

British Library Cataloguing in Publication Data
A catalogue record for this book is available from the British Library

Library of Congress Cataloging in Publication Data
A catalog record has been requested for this book

ISBN10: 0–415–36040–4

ISBN13: 9–78–0–415–36040–1

Contents

Abbreviations

ADD	attention deficit disorder
ADHD	attention deficit hyperactivity disorder
CoPS	Cognitive Profiling System
DCD	developmental co-ordination disorder
DfEE	Department for Education and Employment
DfES	Department for Education and Skills
DVD	developmental verbal dyspraxia
ICT	information and communications technology
LEA	local education authority
PLASC	Pupil Level Annual School Census
PSHCE	personal, social, health and citizenship education
QCA	Qualifications and Curriculum Authority
SEN	special educational needs
SENCO	special educational needs co-ordinator
SENDIST	Special Educational Needs and Disability Tribunal
SNAP	*Special Needs Assessment Portfolio*

Dr Michael Farrell trained as a teacher and as a psychologist at the Institute of Psychiatry and has worked as a head teacher, a lecturer at the Institute of Education, London and as a local education authority inspector. He managed national projects for City University and for the Government Department of Education. Michael Farrell presently works as a special educational consultant. This has involved policy development and training with LEAs, work with voluntary organisations, support to schools in the independent and maintained sectors, and advice to ministries abroad. Among his numerous books, which are translated into European and Asian languages, are:

Key Issues for Primary Schools (Routledge, 1999)

Key Issues for Secondary Schools (Routledge, 2001)

Understanding Special Educational Needs: A Guide for Student Teachers (Routledge, 2003)

Key Issues in Special Education (Routledge, 2005)

Chapter 1

Specific learning difficulties

INTRODUCTION

This chapter sets the book in the context of the 'New Directions in Special Educational Needs' series of which it forms a part. It outlines the contents of the book chapter by chapter and describes the proposed readers. I then define specific learning difficulties and describe pupils considered to have such difficulties. This is done with reference to the *Special Educational Needs Code of Practice* (DfES, 2001a), the guidance *Data Collection by Type of Special Educational Needs* (DfES, 2003) and the legal definition of special educational needs (SEN). The chapter then examines the question of what are considered to be 'specific learning difficulties' and how 'specific' they are. I explain aspects of sensory perception and sensory integration that arise in varying degrees when one comes to consider particular specific learning difficulties.

The sort of provision from which pupils with specific learning difficulties appear to benefit is touched on. Statistics indicating the prevalence of 'specific learning difficulties' in England are presented. The issue of inclusion is examined with particular reference to pupils with specific learning difficulties. I look at the inclusion of pupils already in mainstream schools and the balance of pupils in mainstream and special schools with particular reference to the guidance, *Inclusive Schooling: Children with Special Educational Needs* (DfES, 2001b). Mention is made of the importance of professional liaison, partnership with parents and seeking the views of pupils.

The place of this book in the New Directions in Special Educational Needs series and an outline of chapter contents

This book, *The Effective Teacher's Guide to Dyslexia and Other Specific Learning Difficulties: Practical Strategies*, is part of a 'New Directions in Special Educational Needs' series covering types of SEN related to those outlined in the *Special Educational Needs Code of Practice* (DfES, 2001a). The series focuses on what works in the education of pupils with SEN. It covers:

- behavioural, emotional and social difficulties;
- learning difficulties (moderate, severe, and profound and multiple learning difficulties);
- specific learning difficulties (dyslexia, dyspraxia and dyscalculia);
- communication and interaction difficulties (speech, language and communication difficulties and autistic spectrum disorder);
- sensory and physical difficulties (visual impairment, hearing impairment, multi-sensory impairment and physical disability).

The present book covers:

Chapter 2: Dyslexia: characteristics

This chapter examines definitions of dyslexia with reference to the *Special Educational Needs Code of Practice* (DfES, 2001a), the guidance, *Data Collection by Type of Special Educational Needs* (DfES, 2003), and other sources. I look at estimates of the prevalence of dyslexia and consider literacy difficulties in terms of reading, writing and spelling. The chapter mentions causal factors briefly and these also arise in later sections. I then look at supposed related difficulties (such as phonological difficulties) each in terms of the nature of the difficulty and its identification and assessment. The chapter then considers identification and assessment in connection with liaison between the teacher, the special educational needs co-ordinator (SENCO) and the educational psychologist or other specialist; commercial assessments; and local education authority (LEA) criteria for the statutory assessment of SEN in relation to dyslexia.

Chapter 3: Dyslexia: interventions

This chapter considers interventions predominantly concerning 'associated difficulties' related to dyslexia, that is, interventions such as those for phonological difficulties. I then look at a sample of interventions focusing directly on reading writing and spelling. Finally, two further interventions are examined: developing metacognitive awareness, and identifying and building on strengths (taking account of learning styles and preferred approaches to learning).

Chapter 4: Dyspraxia: its nature and interventions

This chapter explores definitions of dyspraxia and its relationship to developmental co-ordination disorder (DCD). I consider the prevalence of dyspraxia and possible causal factors. The chapter examines some associated underpinning processes: gross and fine motor co-ordination and perceptual-motor development. I look at the identification and assessment of dyspraxia. The chapter outlines some of the difficulties experienced regarding handwriting, physical education and personal and social skills and suggests suitable interventions. Finally, I consider implications for behaviour.

Chapter 5: Dyscalculia: its nature and interventions

This chapter defines dyscalculia and some characteristic difficulties and outlines some of the different types that have been suggested. I look at causal factors and at the identification and assessment of dyscalculia and comment on the difficulty of estimating its prevalence. The chapter explains the prerequisite skills needed to form a basis for mathematics understanding and how the teacher can help the pupil develop them. I discuss some further interventions appropriate for pupils with dyscalculia. The chapter then examines mathematics difficulties associated with dyspraxia and with dyslexia.

Chapter 6: Conclusion

The conclusion considers some of the challenges that remain in developing approaches for specific learning difficulties.

Proposed readers

The book is intended particularly for the following readers:

◆ all teachers, including specialist literacy and numeracy teachers, SENCOs and head teachers in mainstream schools and units working with pupils with specific learning difficulties;
◆ all staff in special schools providing for pupils with specific learning difficulties;
◆ LEA officers, including specialist literacy and numeracy advisers, with an interest in and/or responsibility for pupils with specific learning difficulties;
◆ student teachers and newly qualified teachers wishing to gain an understanding of educational provision for pupils with specific learning difficulties;
◆ teachers and others undergoing continuing professional development;
◆ school advisers and inspectors.

What is specific learning difficulty?

The Special Educational Needs Code of Practice

The *Special Educational Needs Code of Practice* (DfES, 2001a) refers to specific learning difficulties in a section considering 'cognition and learning'. The section also refers to other learning difficulties (moderate, severe and profound) that affect the child more generally and are not therefore specific learning difficulties. The *Code* states:

> Children who demonstrate features of moderate, severe or profound learning difficulties or specific learning difficulties, such as dyslexia or dyspraxia, require specific programmes to aid progress in cognition and learning. Such requirements may also apply to some extent to children with physical and sensory impairments and those on the autistic spectrum. Some of these children may have associated sensory, physical and behavioural difficulties that compound their needs.
>
> (Chapter 7: section 58)

The rather laboured expression, 'demonstrate features of', which evokes images of door-to-door vacuum cleaner vendors, is presumably intended to avoid the possible labelling connotations of the term 'have'. This aside, it will be noted that with regard to specific learning difficulties the examples given are dyslexia (difficulty with reading, writing and spelling and some other difficulties) and dyspraxia (difficulty with acquiring patterns of movement). Pupils with specific learning difficulties will require 'specific programmes', which *may* apply 'to some extent' to children with 'physical and sensory impairments and those on the autistic spectrum'. Furthermore, children with a cognitive and learning difficulty *may* have 'associated sensory, physical and behavioural difficulties'.

Possible triggers for intervention at Early Years Action include, 'the practitioner's or parent's concern about a child who, despite receiving appropriate educational experiences . . . continues working at levels significantly below those expected for children of a similar age in certain areas' (4: 21). In the case of Early Years Action Plus, the triggers for seeking help outside the school could be that, 'despite receiving an individualised programme and/or concentrated support, the child . . . continues to make little or no progress in specific areas over a long period' (4: 31).

In the primary phase, the triggers for School Action could be 'the teacher's or others' concern, underpinned by evidence about a child, who despite receiving differentiated learning opportunities: 'shows signs of difficulty in developing literacy or numeracy skills which result in poor attainment in some curriculum areas' (5: 44). School Action Plus triggers in the primary phase could be that, 'despite receiving an individualised programme and/or concentrated support under School Action, the child . . . continues to have difficulties in developing literacy and numeracy skills' (5: 56).

In the secondary sector, School Action triggers (6: 51) and School Action Plus triggers (6: 64) are almost identical to those for the primary phase.

Regarding the statutory assessment of SEN, when an LEA is deciding whether to carry out an assessment, it should 'seek evidence of any identifiable factors that could impact on learning outcomes including . . . clear, recorded evidence of clumsiness; significant difficulties of sequencing or visual perception; deficiencies in working memory; or significant delays in language functioning' (7: 43).

In the light of evidence about what the *Code* calls the child's 'learning difficulty' but which in fact refers to the child's SEN, the LEA should consider the action taken and particularly should ask whether 'the school has, where appropriate, utilised structured reading and spelling programmes, and multi-sensory teaching strategies to enhance the National Literacy and Numeracy Frameworks' (7: 49).

The guidance Data Collection by Type of Special Educational Needs

A further description of specific learning difficulty is provided in the guidance, *Data Collection by Type of Special Educational Needs*. This is connected with the Pupil Level Annual School Census (PLASC) (DfES, 2003) (www.dfes. gov.uk/sen). The Department for Education and Skills (DfES) sent original draft descriptions to a sample of schools, LEAs and voluntary organisations, and amended them in the light of the comments received. The guidance states:

> Pupils with specific learning difficulties have a particular difficulty in learning
> to read, write and spell or manipulate numbers so that their performance in

these areas is below their performance in other areas. Pupils may also have problems with short-term memory, with organisational skills and with co-ordination. Pupils with specific learning difficulties cover the whole ability range and the severity of their impairment varies widely

(DfES, 2003, p. 3).

Pupils are only recorded as having specific learning difficulties if their difficulties are 'significant and persistent, despite appropriate learning opportunities and if additional educational provision is being made to help them to access the curriculum' (p. 3).

The guidance provides definitions of dyslexia, dyscalculia and dyspraxia. Pupils with dyslexia have 'a marked and persistent difficulty in learning to read, write and spell despite progress in other areas' (p. 3). Children with dyscalculia 'have difficulty in acquiring mathematical skills' (p. 3). Pupils having dyspraxia 'are affected by an impairment or immaturity of the organisation of movement, often appearing clumsy. Gross and fine motor skills are hard to learn and difficult to retain and generalise' (p. 3).

Specific learning difficulties and the legal definition of SEN

Specific learning difficulties can be further understood by examining them in the context of the legal definition of SEN in the Education Act 1996. The Act provides a layered definition in which a 'difficulty in learning' or a 'disability' may lead to a 'learning difficulty', which may call for special educational provision to be made, therefore constituting an SEN. Specific learning difficulty in this context is a 'difficulty in learning' that is significantly greater than that of children of the same age, and that leads to a 'learning difficulty' calling for 'special educational provision'.

Others seem to regard some specific learning difficulties as a disability. For example, Peer and Reid (2003, p. 44), discussing examinations, state, 'Dyslexic learners are allowed specific provisions according to their individual needs. This is intended to give a fair balance for people who have a difficulty in processing information in the same way as their peers due to a disability. Dyslexia is such a disability.'

The language of the PLASC document does not support a view of dyslexia (or dyscalculia) as a disability. Pupils with dyslexia have 'a marked and persistent *difficulty in learning* to read, write and spell despite progress in other areas' (DfES, 2003, p. 3, italics added). Pupils with dyscalculia 'have *difficulty in acquiring* mathematical skills' (p. 3, italics added). Both of these descriptions suggest that both dyslexia and dyscalculia are regarded as a 'difficulty in learning' leading to a 'learning difficulty' that may call for special educational provision. However, the document states that pupils having dyspraxia 'are affected by an *impairment* or immaturity of the organisation of movement, often appearing clumsy. Gross and fine motor skills are hard to learn and difficult to retain and generalise' (p. 3, italics added). This suggests that dyspraxia is seen as a 'disability', leading to a 'learning difficulty' that may call for special educational provision.

What are considered to be the specific learning difficulties?

There is some debate about what 'conditions' are considered to be specific learning difficulties. This book focuses on dyslexia, dyspraxia and dyscalculia, so it may be helpful to explain the rationale behind this as well as to outline some of the areas of debate.

Kirby and Drew (2003, p. 2) pose themselves the question, 'What conditions fall under the label of specific learning difficulties?' They suggest that the conditions include dyslexia, DCD (there is discussion about whether this is different from or the same as dyspraxia) and dyscalculia. They also include Asperger's syndrome, attention deficit hyperactivity disorder (ADHD), deficit of motor perception and dysgraphia. The statement that specific learning difficulties 'include' these seven conditions suggests that others could be added. Indeed, Macintyre and Deponio (2003, pp. 94–9) include 'specific language impairment' (but not dyscalculia).

The conditions that might be considered by others to be specific learning difficulties therefore include:

◆ Asperger's syndrome (a condition on the autistic spectrum);
◆ attention deficit hyperactivity disorder (over-activity and difficulty with maintaining attention);
◆ specific language impairment;
◆ dysgraphia (a difficulty with writing);
◆ deficit of attention and motor perception (difficulty involving attention and movement).

One can see that Asperger's syndrome might be considered to have similarities to specific learning difficulties when it is compared to autism in that it can be seen as differentiated from autism by 'a lack of cognitive delay' (Ayers and Prytis, 2002, p. 22). But when one considers the breadth of functioning affected by Asperger's syndrome, that is, 'social impairment and restricted patterns of behaviour' (p. 22), it is also possible to see it as a broader condition. In this series therefore, Asperger's syndrome is considered within the remit of communication and interaction, not as a specific learning difficulty. This is also the position taken by the document, *Data Collection by Type of Special Educational Needs* (DfES, 2003, p. 6).

Similarly, ADHD might be considered as a specific learning difficulty to the extent that it is not associated directly with a lack of cognitive delay. But neither is behavioural, emotional and social difficulty associated with cognitive delay and this is not usually considered as a specific learning difficulty. In fact there is a strong case for considering ADHD as a behavioural, emotional and social difficulty. This is the view taken in the *Special Educational Needs Code of Practice* (DfES, 2001a, 7.58) and the guidance, *Data Collection by Type of Special Educational Needs* (DfES, 2003, p. 4). Similarly, in this series, I examine ADHD in the book, *The Effective Teacher's Guide to Behavioural, Emotional and Social Difficulties: Practical Strategies*.

Specific language impairment is considered to involve a discrepancy between verbal and non-verbal skills on standardised tests (Macintyre and Deponio, 2003,

p. 99). Given that non-verbal skills are relatively unaffected, the condition may be considered 'specific' to language. As one of the books in this series concerns difficulties with communication and interaction (*The Effective Teacher's Guide to Autism and Communication Difficulties: Practical Strategies*), specific language difficulties are considered there.

Dysgraphia, where there is a difficulty with writing but not generalised learning difficulty, could be considered a specific learning difficulty. Concerning deficit of attention and motor perception, this is a term used mainly in the Scandinavian countries and has areas of overlap with aspects of ADHD and with aspects of dyspraxia. These are not considered in the present book for reasons of space.

How specific are specific learning difficulties?

There are two senses in which one can pose the question, 'how specific are specific learning difficulties?' The first concerns the extent to which some of the conditions do not involve other aspects of intellectual functioning. In considering difficulties in reading, writing and spelling, Martin and Miller (2003, p. 59) make interesting points about differentiating 'specific literacy difficulties' from 'general learning difficulties'. With specific literacy difficulties, 'all other functioning is not giving cause for concern'. But these assumptions, as they indicate, may not be valid (Stanovich, 1994).

The second way in which one can put the question about the specificity of specific learning difficulties concerns the co-occurrence of conditions. A study in Canada (Kaplan *et al.*, 2001) concerned 179 school-aged children assessed for the disorders of dyslexia, dyspraxia, attention deficit disorder (ADD), ADHD, conduct disorders, depression and anxiety. Fifty per cent of the sample was considered to meet the criteria for two or more of the conditions. In Sweden, a study of the 6–7-year-old children in the town of Mariestad identified 10.7 per cent considered to have some kind of neurodevelopmental disorder. All the children with 'deficit of attention and motor perception' had 'developmental co-ordination disorder' and 'attention deficits' (the reader will recognise the conceptual overlap between these). About half met the criteria for ADHD (Gillberg, 1998).

An aspect of the co-occurrence of some of the conditions considered to be specific learning difficulties is the overlap of some of the key difficulties associated with the various conditions. For example, Macintyre and Deponio (2003, p. 7) indicate this in a matrix. They list as specific learning difficulties: dyspraxia, dyslexia, Asperger's syndrome, specific language impairment, ADHD, ADD and deficit of attention and motor perception. They then identify 14 difficulties such as 'literacy' and 'movement fluency' and complete the matrix by showing the existence of many of the difficulties in several conditions. Some conditions are associated with a few of the difficulties while others are linked to many more. For example, ADHD and ADD are associated with 5 of the listed difficulties while dyslexia is linked to 12 and dyspraxia to 11. The co-occurrence of different conditions looks as though it might be to some extent explained by the overlapping of many of the same difficulties in different conditions; for example, every condition is considered to include difficulty with 'social communication'.

At one level, this might suggest that the different conditions are identified according to a series of 'difficulties'. These are common to many of the conditions. Therefore the conditions tend to occur together. In other words, the co-occurrence is simply an artefact of the overlapping way that the conditions are defined. But there is a possibility that other factors might be important. The various common difficulties might suggest elements of common underlying causes of some conditions.

Sensory perception and integration

Sensory perception and integration and specific learning difficulties

An aspect of specific learning difficulties that arises when one considers such difficulties as dyslexia, dyspraxia and dyscalculia is that of sensory perception and integration, which may be implicated in different degrees and in different ways. Some aspects of this are explained below to avoid repeating these when particular conditions are considered in later chapters. In this section, I will consider vestibular sense; auditory discrimination and auditory distractibility; visual discrimination, tracking and field dependence; tactile sense; and proprioceptive/kinaesthetic sense. It is important to remember that these senses and aspects of their functioning work together so that dysfunction in one can affect others.

Vestibular sense

The vestibular system, located in the inner ear, controls one's ability to keep the body balanced when it is in movement and helps the body stay steady when it is not moving. The system monitors the fine-tuning that has to be made so that the body can remain poised even when the environment changes. Because the ability to balance is central to movement and learning, the vestibular sense is extremely important. The system includes, in each ear, three semicircular canals at right angles to each other and connected to a cavity called a vestibule. The canals are lined by hair cells bathed in fluid. Some cells are responsive to gravity and acceleration, while others are sensitive to head movements. Information about position or direction is registered by the respective cells and conveyed by nerve cells to the brain. If the vestibular system is not working properly, the child will have poor sense of balance. His movements will tend to be ungainly, feelings of motion sickness will distort his orientation, and he will tend to have difficulty with directions and poor organisational skills.

Auditory discrimination and auditory distractibility

If a child has difficulties with auditory discrimination, this can involve difficulty in distinguishing sounds (for example 'ch' and 'sh'), which leads to problems with reading and spelling. A child experiencing auditory distractibility may show difficulties in giving attention, concentrating, keeping eye contact and keeping still. Hearing too much in the typically busy classroom environment, he paradoxically has difficulty in listening, that is, focusing on what is pertinent. At the physiological level, the cochlea (auditory apparatus) in the inner ear shares its nerve pathway (the vestibulocochlear nerve) with the vestibular system and the two complement one another.

Visual discrimination, tracking and field dependence

Normally, the eyes function together (convergence) so that a single clear image is conveyed to the brain. The image seen by each eye must be focused and it is mainly the cornea that achieves this. There is also an automatic fine-focusing facility (accommodation), which works by altering the curvature of the eye lens. The magnocellular system relates to the visual discrimination of objects when there is movement, for example when tracking from left to right while reading.

The eyes must be able to scan without losing the clarity of what is seen. If there are problems with convergence and accommodation, then the child may see, for example when looking at a letter of the alphabet, two overlapping or blurred shapes. The implications of this go beyond the obvious impact on reading and writing and also affect the judgement of distance, making sense of other images and other aspects of day-to-day living.

A child with poor visual discrimination may tend to reverse letters when reading and writing, for example reading or writing 'dog' for 'bog'.

Tracking is an important visual skill. It is used, for example, when following the trajectory of a ball while watching or playing a ball game. When estimating distance or direction, as crucially when crossing a road, tracking is vital. It is involved when reading as one follows words across the page or when moving from paragraph to paragraph of a text. When copying words from the board in a classroom, the pupil has the demanding task of tracking words from one plane (the board) to another plane (his writing book). Clearly, difficulties with visual tracking can have a great impact on the education and even the safety of a child.

Regarding field independence and dependence, a child who has good field independence will be able to distinguish items from their background as necessary. A child who is more field dependent than is usual will tend to find it difficult to see items that stand out and find it hard to estimate how much the item projects.

Because vision plays such a central part in maintaining balance, visual difficulties can affect balance, making efficient movement difficult.

Tactile sense

While touch receptors cover the entire body, certain areas such as the mouth and hands are particularly sensitive. Touch enables one to determine a wide range of information about an object; shape and size, texture, weight, malleability, temperature, hardness or softness, and sharpness or bluntness. Through touch, a sense of direction develops, including sidedness or laterality. This aids spatial orientation necessary for balanced movement, which has great importance for learning. Signals from touch receptors pass via sensory nerves to the spinal cord and thence to the thalamus and on to the sensory cortex, where the sensations of touch are perceived and interpreted.

A distinction may be made between protective and discriminatory subsystems of the tactile system. Protective receptors, sensitive, for example, to airwaves passing over the body, indicate when it is appropriate to proceed or withdraw. They help develop a sense of the boundaries of the body, important for dextrous movement such as writing and for arranging items and for judging where the body is in relation to the environment, for example as one is ascending or descending stairs. When the body comes into contact with a person or object, the discriminatory receptors come into play. If protective receptors are too strong, the child may be tactile defensive through a sort of tactile hypersensitivity. This has implications for the child participating in contact sports and for natural physical contact with others. Not receiving cues from being touched can lead to the child having a poor sense of directionality.

Proprioceptive/kinaesthetic sense

The proprioceptive/kinaesthetic sense gives us information about where our body is in space and where parts of the body are in relation to each other and the state of contraction of the muscles. This involves sensory nerve endings within joints, muscles and tendons, and sensory hair cells in the inner ear. Proprioceptors enable movements to be made without looking at the part of the body involved, for example brushing one's hair at the back of the head. When one is moving, information is constantly fed back to the brain from the proprioceptors and the eyes, helping to make sure that movements are co-ordinated and smooth.

Where a child has dysfunctional proprioception, such movements tend to be difficult and the child's perception of depth may also be affected, so that when reaching out for items the child may misjudge and miss or knock the item over. If a child has a dampened proprioceptive sense, he may move excessively to provide the body with information about its position that other children would receive without such effort. The child may appear as fidgety and restless. Proprioceptive difficulties can lead to the child having difficulty using a knife and fork effectively, judging distances and direction when walking to the front of the class and perhaps therefore treading on others and bumping into things. Such difficulties can lower the child's self-esteem if others do not understand the reasons.

Provision for pupils with specific learning difficulties

Later chapters of the book explore provision for pupils with the specific learning difficulties of dyslexia, dyspraxia and dyscalculia. The present section aims to indicate something more about the nature of specific learning difficulties by touching on the interventions that are used when educating pupils with such difficulties.

As a starting point, the *Special Educational Needs Code of Practice* (DfES, 2001a) provides a basic description of provision from which pupils with specific learning difficulties may benefit. However, the possible requirements listed below are intended to apply to pupils with general learning difficulties (moderate, severe or profound) as well as to pupils with specific learning difficulties, so not all can be assumed to apply to the latter.

These children will require some, or all, of the following:

- flexible teaching arrangements
- help with processing language, memory and reasoning skills
- help and support in acquiring literacy skills
- help in organising and co-ordinating spoken and written English to aid cognition
- help with sequencing and organisational skills
- help with problem solving and developing concepts
- programmes to aid improvement of fine and motor competencies
- support in the use of technical terms and abstract ideas
- help in understanding ideas, concepts and experiences when information cannot be gained through first hand sensory and physical experiences.

(DfES, 2001a, 7: 58)

Guidance connected with the PLASC (DfES, 2003) (www.dfes.gov.uk/sen) indicates that pupils should only be recorded as having specific learning difficulties 'if additional educational provision is being made to help them to access the curriculum' (p. 3).

Remembering the overlap of different difficulties associated with some specific conditions, it may be that this suggests that similar interventions might work for different conditions. For example, if a pupil with Asperger's syndrome and a pupil with dyspraxia both experience difficulties with 'social communication', it may be that similar interventions could work with both. However, this may not be so. The apparent cause of the social communication difficulty for the pupil with Asperger's syndrome might be a difficulty with the pragmatics of language (that is the social use of language and related matters). On the other hand, the apparent cause of the social communication difficulty with the pupil with ADHD may be a problem with maintaining attention on the conversation and social overtures of others. If this were so, it suggests that the way of improving the social communication skills of each pupil would be different. In other words, the cause of the difficulty might inform the intervention more than the manifestations of the difficulty.

Causal factors and prevalence of specific learning difficulties

The causal factors related to particular specific learning difficulties (dyslexia, dyscalculia and dyspraxia) and the prevalence of these conditions will be discussed in chapters devoted to each of these difficulties.

There are also statistics relating to specific learning difficulty in which types of difficulty are not specified. Regarding 'specific learning difficulty', in January 2004 in England (DfES, 2004, table 9), there were 60,750 at School Action Plus representing 17.3 per cent of pupils at this part of the SEN framework and a further 23,040 pupils with statements of SEN or 9.8 per cent of pupils with statements.

The figures for ordinary primary and secondary schools and for special schools are as follows. In primary schools, 36,990 of pupils with specific learning difficulty were at School Action Plus (16.9 per cent of all pupils at School Action Plus in primary schools) and 4,790 had statements of SEN (7 per cent of all pupils with statements in primary schools). In secondary schools, the number was 23,750 at School Action Plus (18.1 per cent) and 17,510 with statements of SEN (22.3 per cent). In special schools, where it is much less usual for pupils *not* to have statements of SEN, there were only 10 pupils at School Action Plus (0.7 per cent) and 740 with statements of SEN (0.8 per cent). The figures for special schools included pupils attending maintained and non-maintained special schools but excluded pupils in independent special schools and pupils in maintained hospital schools.

Inclusion and specific learning difficulties

One understanding of inclusion is that it aims to encourage schools to reconsider their structure, teaching approaches, pupil grouping and use of support so that the school responds to the perceived needs of all its pupils. Teachers, collaborating closely, seek opportunities to look at new ways of involving all pupils and to draw on experimentation and reflection. There should be planned access to a broad and balanced curriculum developed from its foundations as a curriculum for all pupils.

Another view of inclusion is that it concerns educating more pupils in mainstream schools and fewer (or none) in special schools and other venues regarded as segregating. However, it may be argued that special schools can also be inclusive (Farrell, 2001, p. 44). Indeed, the Qualifications and Curriculum Authority (QCA) have characterised inclusion as 'securing appropriate opportunities for learning, assessment and qualifications to enable the full and effective participation of all pupils in the process of learning' (Wade, 1999).

A further aspect of inclusion is that of including pupils with SEN who are already in mainstream schools. This approach seems to be the purpose of documents seeking to encourage this kind of inclusion, such as the *Index for Inclusion* (Booth and Ainscow with Black-Hawkins, 2000). The document concerns the inclusion of all those connected with the school, adults as well as children, not only pupils with SEN.

The expression, 'full inclusion', as it applies to pupils with SEN, indicates the view that all pupils with SEN should be educated in mainstream schools. A range of provision in which children with SEN could be educated (such as mainstream school, special school, home tuition) would not be acceptable. It would be better to have increased support and resources in mainstream schools in proportion to the severity and complexity of SEN (e.g. Gartner and Lipsky, 1989). Full inclusion is not the position of the government in England nor is it that of any of the major parties in opposition at the time of writing.

The document, *Inclusive Schooling: Children with Special Educational Needs* (DfES, 2001b), gives statutory guidance on the framework for inclusion. The Special Educational Needs and Disability Act 2001 is said to deliver a 'strengthened right to a mainstream education for children with special educational needs' (p. 1, paragraph 4) by amending the Education Act 1996.

Concerning the nature of the apparent 'right' to inclusion, it is clear that this is constrained. This is indicated by the *Inclusive Schooling* document referring to a 'strengthened right' to mainstream education (p. 1, para. 4). The right (if that is the correct word) is partial. The extent of the right can be seen from the commensurate duties that are placed on others in connection with the 'right'. As a result of the Special Educational Needs and Disability Act 2001, the Education Act 1996 section 316(3) was amended to read:

> If a statement is maintained under section 324 for the child, he must be educated in a mainstream school unless that is incompatible with:
>
> (a) the wishes of his parent, or
>
> (b) the provision of efficient education for other children.

The use of the word, 'must' in the above section of the Act indicates the duty of the LEA and others that corresponds to the 'right' to be educated in the mainstream. If the education of a child with SEN is incompatible with the efficient education of other pupils, mainstream education can only be refused if there are no reasonable steps that can be taken to prevent the incompatibility. But it may not be possible to take steps to prevent a child's inclusion being incompatible with the efficient education of others. This may arise, for example, where the teacher, even with other support, had to spend a greatly disproportionate amount of time with the child in relation to the rest of the class.

The 'rights' are further affected when one considers a particular school rather than the generic concept of 'mainstream'. A parent may express a preference for a particular mainstream school to be named in their child's statement of SEN. In this case, schedule 27 of the Education Act 1996 requires the LEA to name the parents' preferred choice of school in the child's statement unless any of three conditions apply. These are:

1 the school cannot provide for the needs of the child;
2 the child's inclusion at the school would be incompatible with the efficient education of other pupils;
3 the child's inclusion at the school would be incompatible with the efficient use of resources.

It will be seen that there is no comprehensive 'right' of attendance at a mainstream school, but that the rights of the parents of a child with SEN are balanced against the 'rights' of the parents of children who do not have SEN and against other factors. It is in this context that provision – what works best for pupils with specific learning difficulties – should be understood.

Professionals working closely together

Professionals involved with children with specific learning difficulties may include the teacher, the general practitioner, school nurse, school medical officer, the educational psychologist, the physiotherapist and others. Each may have a different professional perspective, and a different level of experience concerning specific learning difficulties.

Among a list of 'barriers' to collaboration listed by Kirby and Drew (2003, p. 85), which is itself selective, are:

◆ staff, time, budget limitations;
◆ competitiveness;
◆ preoccupation with administration;
◆ poor audit and monitoring of services;
◆ logistical issues.

Professional trust is essential, but is difficult to build up where staff turnover is very high. For multi-professional working to be practicable, clear lines of communication are necessary, as is a structure that demarcates responsibility without being too constraining.

Early years development and childcare partnerships use inter-agency planning to bring together early years education and social care. Health action zones and education action zones co-ordinated action on social disadvantage and social support for pupils with SEN. SEN regional partnerships have encouraged discussions and joint planning between education, health and social services on some topics. Aspects of the Excellence in Cities programme included encouraging school-based learning support units working with pupils at risk of exclusion from school to work with learning mentors and out-of-school support services. The Sure Start initiative offered the opportunity to interrelate family policy and the early identification and support of pupils with SEN.

In 2003, an Early Support Pilot Programme was designed to develop good service provision and to support development in various areas including the co-ordination of multi-agency support for families and partnership across agencies and geographical boundaries. This involved joint work between the DfES and others, including the Royal National Institute for the Blind, the Royal National Institute for the Deaf and the National Children's Bureau (www.earlysupport.org.uk). See also the DfES website (www.dfes.gov.uk/sen), the Department of Health website (www.doh.gov.uk) or the National Children's Bureau website (www.ncb.org.uk).

Related to joint professional working, a National Children's Trust Framework was announced in 2001 intended to develop new standards across the National Health Service and social services for children and encourage partnership between agencies. Children's Trusts were subsequently seen as seeking to integrate local education, social care and some health services (through the Health Act 1999, section 31) for children and young people and incorporate an integrated commissioning strategy. The LEA will include potentially all education functions including SEN, the education welfare service and educational psychology. Children's social services will include assessment and services for children 'in need'. Community and acute health services will include locally provided and commissioned child and adolescent mental health services and could also include speech and language therapy, health visiting and occupational therapy services concerned with children and families. (Primary Care Trusts will be able to delegate functions into the Children's Trust and will be able to pool funds with the local authority.)

Trusts can also include other services such as Connexions and Sure Start. Other local partners such as the police, voluntary organisations, housing services and leisure services can be involved. Children's Trusts are expected to sit within local authorities reporting to the director of children's services, who in turn will report to the chief executive to the local councillors. The Children's Trusts will commission services and may provide these directly or by contracts through public, private or voluntary sector organisations.

The resulting integration of service provision is expected to be reflected in such features as: collocated services such as Children's Centres and extended schools; multi-disciplinary teams and a key worker system; a common assessment framework across services; information-sharing systems across services; joint training; and effective arrangements for safeguarding children. The intention is to integrate key children's services within a single organisational focus, preferably through Children's Trusts, which it was envisaged would exist in most areas by 2006. Bids for 35 'Pathfinder' Trusts were approved in 2003, funded to 2006 (www.doh.gov.uk/nsf/children/index.htm).

Working with parents

Working closely with parents is an aspiration of all schools and a continuing theme in government guidance. The *Special Educational Needs Code of Practice* (DfES, 2001a) devotes a chapter to 'Working in Partnership with Parents' and specific guidance on seeking to understand what parents need is available (e.g. Greenwood, 2002). The school's support of parents may include:

- providing information about SEN and practical strategies for coping;
- putting parents in touch with support groups locally and nationally;
- making school premises available for various activities, such as a parents' support group;
- having displays of literature, such as leaflets;
- being a 'one stop' point of contact for other services.

A model for collaborating with parents in order to help pupils experiencing difficulties at school is suggested by Hornby (2003, p. 131), which may have wider application for work with parents of pupils with SEN more generally. It distinguishes between what parents are considered to 'need' and what they can reasonably be expected to contribute.

Parents *needs* are considered to be for communication with the school (which all parents need); liaison such as that taking place at parent–teacher meetings (which most parents need); education such as parents' workshops (which many need); and support such as counselling (which some need).

Parents' *contributions* are considered as information, for example about the child's strengths (which all parents can provide); collaboration, for example with behaviour programmes or supporting a pupil's individual education plans (to which most parents could contribute); resources, such as being a classroom aid (which many could contribute); and helping develop policy, for example being a parent governor of the school (which some could contribute).

The model leaves open the exact interpretation of what the expressions 'most', 'many' and 'some' might mean and schools will bring their own judgements to bear on, for example, whether it is reasonable to expect 'many' parents to contribute at a level suggested by being a classroom aid. Nevertheless the basic structure of the model with a graduated view of the parents' proposed needs and the contribution is a helpful one.

Pupils' views

Lewis (2004) lists some aspects of methods relevant to chronologically young children or 'developmentally young' children. These include:

- permit or encourage 'don't know' responses and requests for clarification;
- stress not knowing the events or views of the child to counter the child's assumption that the adult knows the answer (the child tends to be more suggestible if the adult has credibility and rapport with the child);
- use statements rather than questions to trigger fuller responses from children;
- if using question, use an appropriate level of generality (for example, 'open or moderately focused questions seem to generate more accurate responses from children with learning difficulties than do highly specific questions');
- avoid 'yes/no' questions to avoid acquiescence, particularly for pupils with learning difficulties; and
- aim for an uninterrupted narrative.

(Lewis, 2004, pp. 4–6 paraphrased)

The *Special Educational Needs Code of Practice* (DfES, 2001a, especially chapter 3) encourages pupil participation and seeks to involve pupils with specific learning difficulty in the development and evaluations of the individual education plan. A balance is sought between encouraging participation and over-burdening the pupil when he may not have sufficient experience and knowledge to make judgements without support.

THINKING POINT

Readers may wish to consider:

- the problems of defining specific learning difficulties as a group of conditions.

KEY TEXT

Macintyre, C. and Deponio, P. (2003) *Identifying and Supporting Children with Specific Learning Difficulties: Looking Beyond the Label to Assess the Whole Child*, London, RoutledgeFalmer.

This book focuses on the range of 'indicators' that are associated with various specific learning difficulties and the extent to which they appear to overlap. This leads the authors to suggest that practitioners look beyond any label such as dyspraxia or dyslexia and recognise and provide for possible underlying or associated difficulties.

Chapter 2

Dyslexia

Characteristics

INTRODUCTION

This chapter examines definitions of dyslexia with reference to the *Special Educational Needs Code of Practice* (DfES, 2001a), the guidance, *Data Collection by Type of Special Educational Needs* (DfES, 2003), and other sources. I look at estimates of the prevalence of dyslexia and consider literacy difficulties in terms of reading, writing and spelling. I mention causal factors briefly as these also arise in later sections. The chapter then looks at supposed related difficulties each in terms of the nature of the difficulty and the identification and assessment of the difficulty. I examine phonological difficulties; auditory perception and auditory processing difficulties; visual difficulties and visual processing difficulties; motor co-ordination difficulties; short-term verbal memory difficulties; and sequencing difficulties. I then consider identification and assessment in connection with liaison between the teacher, the SENCO and the educational psychologist or other specialist; commercial assessments; and LEA criteria for the statutory assessment of SEN in relation to dyslexia.

Defining and describing dyslexia

A definition of dyslexia developed by the British Psychological Society (1999) is that: 'Dyslexia is evident when accurate and fluent word reading and/or spelling develops very incompletely or with great difficulty' (p. 18). But this is only one of many attempts to define the condition. Keates (2000), in a book concerning information and communications technology (ICT) and dyslexia, disarmingly admits, 'In the course of researching this book, I have tried to find a single, agreed definition of dyslexia. However, after discovering 28 different ones and not even exhausting my search, I gave up' (p. 1).

To try to make sense of the plethora of definitions, this section examines the understanding of dyslexia suggested by the *Special Educational Needs Code of Practice* (DfES, 2001a) and the guidance, *Data Collection by Type of Special Educational Needs* (DfES, 2003). It then looks at discrepancy views of dyslexia and at other definitions of dyslexia in terms of literacy difficulties and in terms of supposed associated difficulties.

The Special Educational Needs Code of Practice

As indicated in the previous chapter, the *Special Educational Needs Code of Practice* (DfES, 2001a) refers to specific learning difficulties in a section considering 'cognition and learning'. The *Code* states: 'Children who demonstrate features of . . . specific learning difficulties, such as dyslexia . . . require specific programmes to aid progress in cognition and learning. . . . Some of these children may have associated sensory, physical and behavioural difficulties that compound their needs' (7: 58).

It will be remembered that possible triggers for intervention at the level of Early Years Action include 'the practitioner's or parent's concern about a child who, despite receiving appropriate educational experiences . . . continues working at levels significantly below those expected for children of a similar age in certain areas' (4: 21). In the case of Early Years Action Plus, the triggers for seeking help outside the school could be that 'despite receiving an individualised programme and/or concentrated support, the child . . . continues to make little or no progress in specific areas over a long period' (4: 31).

In the primary phase, the triggers for School Action could be 'the teacher's or others' concern, underpinned by evidence about a child, who, despite receiving differentiated learning opportunities, 'shows signs of difficulty in developing literacy or numeracy skills which result in poor attainment in some curriculum areas' (5: 44). School Action Plus triggers in the primary phase could be that, 'despite receiving an individualised programme and/or concentrated support under School Action, the child . . . continues to have difficulties in developing literacy and numeracy skills' (5: 56). In the secondary sector, School Action triggers (6: 51) and School Action Plus triggers (6: 64) are almost identical to those for the primary phase.

Regarding the statutory assessment of SEN, when an LEA is deciding whether to carry out an assessment, it should 'seek evidence of any identifiable factors that could impact on learning outcomes including . . . clear, recorded evidence of clumsiness; significant difficulties of sequencing or visual perception; deficiencies in working memory; or significant delays in language functioning' (7: 43). The LEA should consider the action taken and particularly should ask whether 'the school has, where appropriate, utilised structured reading and spelling programmes, and multi-sensory teaching strategies to enhance the National Literacy and Numeracy Frameworks' (7: 49).

The guidance, Data Collection by Type of Special Educational Needs, *and discrepancy views*

A description of dyslexia is provided in *Data Collection by Type of Special Educational Needs*, a document offering guidance connected with the PLASC (DfES, 2003) (www.dfes.gov.uk/sen). It will be remembered that pupils are only recorded as having specific learning difficulties if their difficulties are 'significant and persistent, despite appropriate learning opportunities and if additional educational provision is being made to help them to access the curriculum' (p. 3). The guidance states:

Pupils with dyslexia have a marked and persistent difficulty in learning to read, write and spell despite progress in other areas. Pupils may have poor reading comprehension, handwriting and punctuation. They may also have difficulties in concentration and organisation and in remembering sequences of words. They may mispronounce common words or reverse letters and sounds in words.

(p. 3)

The definition just considered provides an opportunity to examine the question of a discrepancy view of dyslexia. A discrepancy view defines reading impairment in terms of a discrepancy between a child's actual reading score and the reading score that would be predicted on the basis of chronological age or IQ (or both). Normally, discrepancy scores are defined as the difference between the score on a specified reading test and the score predicted from the regression of reading performance on a measure of IQ (that is the correlation between reading and IQ). A discrepancy of a specified value is taken to be a measure of underachievement in reading.

If pupils with specific learning difficulty cover the 'whole ability range' as indicated in the guidance, *Data Collection by Type of Special Educational Needs* (DfES, 2003, p. 3), this will include some pupils who are very able. An indication of this would be high performance in areas of the curriculum where their specific learning difficulty has less impact than others. If this were not so, and attainment was low in many areas, the learning difficulty would be considered not specific but general as in the case of moderate, severe or profound learning difficulty.

This raises the important question of whether a pupil could be considered to have dyslexia if he is performing at a level equal to that of children of the same age but on the basis of IQ predictions would normally be expected to be doing even better. In this context, Pollock *et al.* (2004) state:

A match in reading age and chronological age does not necessarily rule out a reading problem. A bright child should be capable of scoring a reading age even two years ahead of the standardised average of his chronological age. The criterion to be looked at should always be the *discrepancy* between performance and the potential to satisfy his intellectual needs.

(p. 53, italics added)

It is not clear in the above extract whether the authors are talking about a special educational need, because they use the phrase, 'reading problem'. But Miles and Miles (1990, p. iv) are quite unequivocal, going so far as to claim that 'there is no contradiction in saying that a person is dyslexic while never the less being a competent reader'. Even Beaton, in a book distinguished by its impartiality, recognises that this is a 'provocative claim' (Beaton, 2004, p. 9).

Dykman and Ackerman (1992) take a view more conversant with modern-day thinking:

Regression formulas are well and good if the purpose is to identify all students who are underachievers. But it defies common sense to diagnose the child with an IQ of 130 and a reading standard score of 110 as having dyslexia. Certainly the public school system should not be expected to offer special services to such a child.

(p. 574)

In line with the views of such writers as Dykman and Ackerman (1992), a pupil defined in the discrepancy way they describe would not be considered to have a specific learning difficulty as understood in the PLASC guidance (DfES, 2003). This is because the guidance allows pupils to be recorded as having specific learning difficulties only if their difficulties are 'significant and persistent, despite appropriate learning opportunities and if additional educational provision is being made to help them to access the curriculum' (p. 3). It would be difficult to argue that a pupil had difficulties with literacy that were 'significant and persistent' if their performance in literacy is age average. Similarly, it is hard to understand how pupils with dyslexia can have 'a marked and persistent difficulty in learning to read, write and spell despite progress in other areas' (p. 3) if the pupil performed as well as other pupils of the same age in similar conditions.

Other definitions of dyslexia

When looking at attempts to describe and define dyslexia, it seems odd to come across perspectives that present reading, writing and spelling difficulties as apparently being only *conditional* characteristics of dyslexia. Peer and Reid (2003) suggest:

> Children with dyslexia will *usually, but not always*, have difficulty with reading.
>
> (p. 9, italics added)

> . . . spelling difficulties are *often* an obvious characteristic of dyslexia.
>
> (p. 10, italics added)

> Children with dyslexia *may* also have difficulties with both expressive writing and their actual handwriting style.
>
> (p. 10, italics added)

They also state that:

> *Many* people consider those who are dyslexic to have a problem which is solely about reading. We know that this is absolutely not the case. Some people do have such a weakness, yet others do not. *All* seem to have a problem, however, with part of the writing process.
>
> (p. 41, italics added)

Taken together, this appears to imply that a child with dyslexia:

- *usually* has difficulties with reading (but may not);
- *often* has spelling difficulties (but may not);

- *may* have difficulties with writing (but may not);
- *always* seems to have a problem with part of the writing process.

So is one way to make sense of these apparently conditional characteristics of dyslexia to assume that at least one of the difficulties is evident: either reading, writing or spelling? Leaving aside the question of what seeming to have a problem with 'part of the writing process' might mean, this would imply that most children with dyslexia have difficulty with reading and that those who do not have a difficulty with either writing or spelling or both. This seems to be the case when one examines some of the definitions of dyslexia.

The British Dyslexia Association definition is:

> a combination of *abilities and difficulties which affect the learning process* in one or more of **reading, spelling and writing**. Accompanying weaknesses may be identified in areas of speed processing, short-term memory, sequencing, auditory and/or visual perception, spoken language and motor skills. It is particularly related to mastering and using written language, which may include alphabetic, numeric and musical notation.
>
> (Peer, 2001, bold and italics added)

The definition developed in the Republic of Ireland by the Government Task Force on Dyslexia (www.irlgov.ie/educ/pub.htm) is, 'Dyslexia is manifested in a continuum of specific learning *difficulties related to the acquisition* of basic skills in **reading, spelling and/or writing**, such difficulties being unexpected in relation to an individual's other abilities and educational experiences' (Task Force on Dyslexia, 2001, bold and italics added).

Peer and Reid, after reviewing similar definitions, observe that '[t]hese definitions support the view that dyslexia relates to a *broad range of difficulties* associated with **literacy** and learning' (2003, p. 14, bold and italics added).

Two perspectives can be taken of definitions such as those above. The first emphasises the manifestations of reading, writing and spelling as highlighted in bold in the definitions. In this perspective, dyslexia *is* the difficulty with reading, writing and spelling indicated by lower than age average attainment in literacy. The second view emphasises the possible difficulties that appear to be associated with low literacy attainment. These are indicated in italic script in the definitions cited above. They are such features as the 'abilities and difficulties which affect the learning process', 'difficulties related to the acquisition of basic skills', and the 'broad range of difficulties associated with literacy'. To the extent that these difficulties are highlighted, it is almost as if *they* are what dyslexia really is and lower than age average literacy skills are their consequences or manifestations.

Related to this, one can ask whether a pupil once assessed as having dyslexia can progress to an extent that he is no longer considered to have dyslexia. This might seem a strange question at first. If one asked if a pupil with literacy difficulties could progress so as to no longer be considered to have literacy difficulties the answer would be affirmative. But, for pupils with dyslexia, supposed associated factors enter the picture. If, for example, a child has associated difficulties with information processing, can these be considered to persist after strategies have been developed to enable the child to gain literacy skills equal in all respects to children of the same age? The answer may be that such difficulties could still exist. Even so the child cannot be said to 'have' dyslexia, if the central aspect of dyslexia is literacy difficulties. One may want to find another term to indicate that the pupil may experience information processing difficulties, and one would want to be aware of these in the child's teaching and learning, but one could not say that the child had dyslexia.

The pupil no longer has 'difficulties related to the acquisition of basic skills in reading, spelling and/or writing' because these skills have been acquired, unless one is to see the difficulties (e.g. information processing) as dyslexia.

This book focuses on the SEN perspective of dyslexia in that dyslexia is seen as evidenced by a child having lower than age average attainment in literacy when compared with children of the same age under similar conditions (for example where children are given the same period of time to complete a literacy task).

Prevalence

Prevalence in relation to SEN refers to the number of children with a particular type of SEN in a specified population over a specified period, for example 0–5 years old or school age. Incidence is usually expressed as the number of children per live births in a given year. Prevalence is related to incidence in that prevalence is determined by the incidence of a condition and its duration (see also Farrell, 2003, pp. 129–30).

Estimates of the prevalence of dyslexia vary. Developmental dyslexia has been said to affect about 5 per cent of the global population (Ramus, 2001, p. 393). Estimates of prevalence in the English-speaking world fall between 5 and 10 per cent of the population (Pennington, 1990).

Characteristics of literacy difficulties

Reading difficulties and their identification and assessment

The pupil's difficulties in reading may include certain characteristics. The child may:

◆ *hesitate over words*;
◆ *confuse* – letters with similar shapes such as 'u' and 'n';
            – visually similar words such as 'was' and 'saw';
            – small words such as 'it' and 'is';
◆ *omit* – small words such as 'it' and 'is', other words, word endings;
◆ *make errors regarding* – semantically related words, for example reading 'cat' for 'dog';
            – polysyllabic words such as 'animal', 'corridor', 'family' and so on;
            – grammar, including the inconsistent use of tense.

The identification and assessment of difficulties with reading is likely to include:

◆ a profile of the sorts of errors that the pupil makes (see the characteristics of reading difficulties above), for example using miscue analysis (e.g. Pollock *et al.*, 2004, pp. 54–8);

- an indication of how the pupil reads (e.g. whether he is hesitant over words);
- an indication of whether the pupil tends to prefer silent reading or reading aloud and whether one leads to fewer mistakes than the other.

Writing difficulties and their identification and assessment

The child may:

- be reluctant to write;
- have particular difficulty copying writing from the board and find it easier to copy from material on his desk or table;
- have an inconsistent handwriting style.

The identification and assessment of difficulties with writing is likely to include:

- the pupil's approach to writing tasks (e.g. reluctance);
- whether copying from the board appears particularly difficult;
- the consistency of the child's handwriting style.

Spelling difficulties and their identification and assessment

The child may have difficulties with:

- the words endings 'er', 'or' and 'ar', for example spelling 'paper' as 'papor' or papar';
- commonly used words as well as less frequently used ones;
- certain sounds such 's' and 'z'.

He or she may tend to:

- spell phonetically (for example, 'fotograf' for 'photograph');
- omit the middle or end of a word;
- spell certain words inconsistently ('nesesery', 'nececary', 'nesacary' and so on for 'necessary');
- write letters or syllables in the wrong sequence.

The identification and assessment of a pupil's difficulty with spelling will include a profile of the sorts of errors made by the pupil (see the characteristics of spelling difficulties above).

Causal factors

Given that the definitions of dyslexia are often conditional and given the complicated nature of acquiring literacy skills and understanding, it is hardly surprising that there is debate about possible causal factors, which may vary in relation to the particular nature and extent of the literacy difficulty. In so-called exclusionary definitions, dyslexia is not considered to be caused by general intellectual impairment hence its designation as a specific not a general learning difficulty. Neither is it considered that it is brought about by sociocultural constraints or by emotional factors.

Among the factors associated with dyslexia are phonological difficulties, difficulties with information processing, memory and co-ordination, organisational difficulties, problems with sequencing and orientation, visual difficulties and auditory processing difficulties. Each of these is considered in the next section as 'possible associated difficulties'. Each of the 'associated difficulties' in varying degrees can be seen as explaining something about literacy problems. For example, if a child has phonological difficulties, that is, problems with sound-related aspects of language, then the relationships between this and written or read text is likely to be problematic. At one level then, such associated factors can be said to contribute to literacy difficulties (although the relationship may be reciprocal).

Another level of explanation arises when one considers how the 'associated difficulties' might have arisen. What has caused or contributed to phonological difficulties? What led to problems with information processing? Sometimes in connection with such issues, biological explanations are offered.

Possible associated difficulties and their identification and assessment

Phonological difficulties

Phonetics (the study of articulation), prosody (concerned with features of speech such as volume and patterns of intonation) and phonology are interrelated aspects of speech. Phonology has to do with the 'meaningful contrast of speech sounds' (Martin and Miller, 2003, p. 38). When a child's speech difficulty concerns phonology there is a difficulty in relating speech sounds to changes in meaning. Phonological knowledge enables the speaker to understand that, when a speech sound is changed in a word, meaning changes. Speakers normally come to learn distinctions (e.g. 'dog'/'log' or 'pig'/'pin') and the speaker, hearing her own speech, modifies it as necessary to make the required word. The phonological system is considered to lay down a sort of phonological representation of the speech sound sequence at a 'cognitive level of language functioning' (Martin, 2000, p. 14), which helps the process to be automatic. Speakers can then draw on this phonological representation when they are developing awareness of the different sounds in a word. In reading in English, the 44 speech sounds are linked to written marks or graphemes so that the child develops a phoneme–grapheme correspondence.

The phonological deficit theory maintains that in dyslexia the main cognitive deficit is in a person's ability to represent or recall speech sounds (phonemes), that is, there is a problem with phonological representations. This phonological deficit leads to the poor mental mapping of letters of the alphabet to phonemes. Both the phonological deficit and the poor letter–phoneme mapping operate at the cognitive level but have implications at the behavioural level, where both lead to difficulties with phonological tasks such as splitting words into their phonemes. Also, poor letter–phoneme mapping relates to reading difficulties.

Among extensive evidence in support of the phonological deficit theory is that people with dyslexia have difficulty retaining speech in short-term memory and consciously breaking it up into phonemes. For example, a person with dyslexia will tend to have difficulty deleting or substituting phonemes from words (Snowling, 2000). A phonological deficit in children at the age of 6 years was found in a Norwegian study to be a strong predictor of reading difficulties (Hagtvet, 1997). Speech rate has also been identified as a predictor of dyslexic difficulties (e.g. Hulme and Snowling, 1997). A double deficit of phonological processing and naming speed has been suggested (e.g. Wolf and O'Brien, 2001). Cerebellar impairment may be implicated with dyslexia and may be linked to phonological processing (and balance) (Fawcett et al., 1996).

Briefly, because, in an alphabetical system, the brain has to map letters of the alphabet on to mental representations of the corresponding phonemes, problems representing and recalling phonemes is expected to lead to reading difficulties. However, the exact nature of the phonological deficit and its biological cause is not yet fully understood.

The identification and assessment of phonological difficulties is likely to include assessing:

◆ whether the child's expressive language includes errors, omissions or other difficulties in conversation or in classroom interaction (suggesting that there may be difficulties relating to key meaningful elements of sound);
◆ whether the child has difficulty with the comprehension of speech, for example not appearing to understand instructions or questions (suggesting that the child may have difficulty with the elements of speech that convey meaning).

As well as identifying difficulties, the assessment can provide information that can later suggest strategies that will help the child's learning or identify strategies that the child has already developed. For example, the assessment could indicate what mode of 'input' (verbal, written or visual) appears to aid comprehension. This might indicate a preference for visual input that might to some degree help aid comprehension where there are phonological difficulties. Or the child's expressive language can be observed in different contexts to see if he finds communication easier in some contexts than in others.

Auditory perception and auditory processing difficulties

Given that some perceptual aspects of speech are relevant to developing phonemic awareness, it has been proposed that reading ability may be related to speech perception. One aspect of auditory perception concerns so-called phonetic categorisation. In making different speech sounds, there are different durations between the instant that air is released from the lips and the vocal chords vibrating, which is known as the 'voice-onset time', important as a cue in speech perception. Presenting sounds using a speech synthesiser, with a 0 millisecond voice-onset time, produces a perception of a /ba/ sound. A 40 millisecond voice-onset time leads to a perception of a /pa/ sound. At voice-onset times between 0 and 40 msec., people report hearing either a /ba/ or a /pa/ sound, not a sound somewhere between the two, a phenomenon called 'categorical perception'.

Some children with dyslexia have been found to be 'less consistent' in their classification of stimuli and changed more gradually than did a control group of children from one phonetic category to another (Godfrey *et al.*, 1981, p. 419). It was suggested that this inconsistency in phonic categorisation might impair the ability of a child with dyslexia to learn through forming 'inadequate long-term representations of phonetic units' (p. 420). This could adversely affect reading processes involving 'the transformation of script to phonetic units of speech, as well as the ordering and combining of those units that make up words' (p. 420).

Other auditory processing impairments have been found in some people with dyslexia using electrophysiological techniques. Adults with dyslexia were found to be less sensitive as a group to amplitude changes in sound stimuli than a control group despite all participants having hearing thresholds of 15 dB or better. Amplitude modulation in speech helps its intelligibility, so dyslexic listeners were considered to be impaired in their identification of speech (Menell, *et al.*, 1999, p. 802).

The identification of auditory processing difficulties is likely to involve identifying:

◆ difficulties with auditory discrimination;
◆ inability to perceive consonant sounds in different positions (initial, medial, final);
◆ difficulties with auditory sequencing;
◆ difficulties with auditory blending;
◆ difficulties with auditory segmentation.

Visual difficulties and visual processing difficulties

Scotopic sensitivity (Irlen, 1994) is a term that has come to be used to refer to a particular sensitivity to black print on white paper. Helen Irlen found that some students in high school and at university in the United States of America who were poor readers had a particular sensitivity to black print on white paper, especially where the print was faint, the paper was glossy and fluorescent lighting was used. Words appeared to move around the page and the glare from the page tended to cause eye irritation. For some pupils, spectacles with tinted lenses or coloured page overlays appear to help reduce the glare and stabilise the image of the words on the page.

Other visual factors that may be associated with dyslexia relate to convergence, accommodation and tracking. Convergence is a skill necessary to effective reading, writing and spelling (and of course other activities) and involves the eyes converging on the letters of print or handwriting at a distance of about 30 centimetres to ensure that the brain receives a unified picture of the letters and words. For some children with dyslexia, it has been suggested that there may be difficulties with the vision converging, which can lead to binocular instability (Stein, 1995). Accommodation relates to the skill of being able to quickly adjust the focus of the eyes to changing circumstances, such as the changing distances between print and the eye as the eye moves down a page of writing. Where there are problems with accommodation, clearly reading, writing and spelling are likely to be affected. Tracking concerns the skill of scanning a line of print from word to word and from line to line while keeping one's place. Where there is a difficulty with this, the pupil will tend to loose his place easily when reading.

Nevertheless, Beaton (2004) states that 'The general consensus in the literature, however, appears to favour the view that abnormal eye movements are a consequence rather than a cause of reading disability' (p. 219).

Some people with dyslexia seem to have difficulties with visual tasks, such as those involving the perception of movement. One attempt to explain such findings is the magnocellular theory. (There are also proposed auditory aspects of the theory but the focus here is on the visual). The magnocellular theory is based on the division of the visual system into two neuronal pathways: the magnocellular pathway and the parvocellular pathway. It is hypothesised that the proposed magnocellular system is abnormal in people with dyslexia. This causes difficulties in some aspects of visual perception and in binocular control that may lead to a reading difficulty. Impaired development of the magnocellular component of the visual system, which processes fast temporal information, may lead to visual confusions such as letters looking blurred or appearing to move around (e.g. Stein *et al.*, 2001).

Therefore, at the neurological level, there is considered to be a general magnocellular dysfunction. This leads to a visual magnocellular deficit and a temporal auditory deficit at the cognitive level. (The temporal auditory deficit is believed to lead to the phonological deficit). At the behavioural level, the visual magnocellular deficit is hypothesised to lead to difficulties with certain visual tasks, such as those requiring the perception of motion, and to reading difficulties. The temporal auditory deficit is thought to lead to, at the behavioural level, difficulties with certain auditory tasks requiring the perception of brief or rapid speech (or non-speech) sounds.

The assessment of visual difficulties is likely to involve assessing that the pupil:

◆ has age-inappropriate difficulty discriminating between letters that appear the same ('m' and 'n');
◆ has age-inappropriate difficulty discriminating between letters that are the same but have different forms ('M' and 'm');
◆ omits or transposes part of a word (which could indicate a difficulty with visual segmentation).

Motor co-ordination difficulties

Some children with dyslexia have difficulties with motor co-ordination affecting handwriting and other fine motor skills, as well as gross motor skills as used in daily life and that are particularly evident in some sports.

Haslum (1989) considered two tests of gross motor co-ordination that were part of the British Birth Cohort Study. The first was to catch a ball, throw it into the air while clapping the hands a specified number of times, then catching it again. The second test involved walking backwards along a straight line. Failure on these two tests was associated with membership of a group of children defined as dyslexic at the age of 10 years (in part according to underachievement in reading and spelling).

Some dyslexic children have difficulties with fine motor skills as reported in several studies (see examples in Beaton 2004, pp. 128–30). It has been suggested that, under conditions where demands are made requiring attention to be allocated to different tasks, a person with dyslexia may be disadvantaged. This is because he is unable to perform certain tasks such as balancing automatically and consequently has to allocate particular attention to this while others for whom such activities are automatic do not (e.g. Fawcett and Nicholson, 1992).

The identification and assessment of co-ordination difficulties is likely to include a profile of the areas and circumstances in which these difficulties are apparent, such as poor handwriting and difficulty with a range of other fine motor tasks as well as gross motor activities.

Short-term verbal memory difficulties

Problems with verbal memory and learning have been found in many studies of dyslexia, particularly in tasks requiring phonological processes (Share, 1995). For example, many studies have found that children with dyslexia tend to have lower digit spans than control readers (e.g. McDougal et al., 1994). One possibility is that difficulties with verbal memory in some children with dyslexia relate to difficulties in phonological awareness because memory difficulties contribute to problems in keeping in mind individual phonemes as part of a phonic reading strategy (Beaton, 2004, p. 72).

Other research suggests that good readers are more likely to use verbal retrieval or rehearsal strategies than are poor readers. Poor readers may use visually based strategies more than good readers (e.g. Palmer, 2000). Memory span for verbal items is longer for words than for pseudo-words of the same length, suggesting that, when remembering lists of items, it is easier to remember words from established representations in long-term memory. It has been suggested (Hulme et al., 1997) that a partially decayed memory trace may be reconstructed from stored knowledge about the structure of words. If, for people with dyslexia, this knowledge were inefficiently represented, it would not be as helpful as otherwise in supporting the process of reconstruction, resulting in lower recall performance in people with dyslexia.

The identification and assessment of memory difficulties is likely to include a profile of the areas and circumstances in which these difficulties are apparent. As well as its effect on reading and related activities, poor short-term memory may be indicated by difficulty in remembering instructions, sequences of numbers, facts and dates, and appointments and deadlines for work. Naturally, the child will find it more difficult to process information in short-term memory if he is trying to do something else at the same time or if distracted. The teacher might find it informative to note the strategies that the pupil already has to aid memory in a broader sense and that appear to work, such as a diary or computer software that help the pupil plan and remind him of deadlines.

Sequencing difficulties (temporal order)

Several studies have indicated that poor readers are less able than average or good readers to remember the serial order of events. For example, in a study by

Corkin (1974), participants were required to reproduce a sequence of taps on a wooden block or were required to repeat a sequence of digits. A relationship was found between the accuracy of recall of a sequence of events and reading attainment.

A 'temporal processing deficit' has been proposed that might involve a 'high degree of processing overlap associated with the parallel transmission of speech' (Share, 1995, p. 188), which could lead to poor phonological representations. Such a deficit could also explain difficulties in 'the rapid sequencing of speech motor acts necessary for serial naming and verbal rehearsal' (p. 188).

Beaton (2004) summarises such findings as strongly suggesting 'some anomaly in the temporal aspects of auditory system dysfunction of dyslexics which is likely to have an impact on phonological skills and hence reading' (p. 127).

Identifying sequencing difficulties is likely to involve identifying difficulties with the child:

◆ sequencing information (e.g. sequencing letters of the alphabet, words when reading, letters in writing, numbers or remembering telephone numbers);
◆ sequencing chronological events (e.g. sequencing days of the week and months of the year or recalling a sequence of events).

It is helpful to develop a profile of the difficulties the child experiences (see above) and note, for example, when a pupil *is* able to follow sequences of instructions and what support is required.

Other aspects of identification and assessment

The teacher, the SENCO and the educational psychologist

The classroom teacher in a primary school and perhaps teachers of English in secondary school may be well placed to notice difficulties with literacy that might suggest investigating whether a pupil has dyslexia. Observations would include gathering information on difficulties with reading, writing and spelling. These were outlined earlier and will not be repeated here.

Where a teacher has concerns about a pupil's attainment and progress, the SENCO would be consulted and she might gather further information. It is important that information on the pupil's performance in reading, writing and spelling be noted in different settings such as whole class, small groups and for different subjects of the curriculum. Should concerns persist, the SENCO may consult others as appropriate, such as an educational psychologist.

Commercial assessments

Among commercial assessments of dyslexia are the following, which, it will be noticed, sample aspects of some of the supposed associated difficulties already examined.

◆ The *Dyslexia Early Screening Test – Junior* (Fawcett and Nicholson, 2004a) is intended for children aged 6 years, 6 months to 11 years, 5 months and is administered individually, taking about 30 minutes. Its sub-tests comprise: rapid naming; bead threading; one-minute reading; postural stability; phonemic segmentation; two-minute spelling; backwards digit span; nonsense passage reading; one-minute writing; verbal fluency; rhyme; and receptive vocabulary.

◆ The *Dyslexia Screening Test – Secondary* (Fawcett and Nicholson, 2004b) is for children and young people aged 11 years, 8 months to 16 years, 5 months and is administered individually taking about 30 minutes. Its sub-tests are: rapid naming; threading beads; one-minute reading; postural stability; phonemic segmentation; two-minute spelling; backwards digit span; reading a nonsense passage; one-minute writing; verbal fluency; semantic fluency; spoonerisms; and non-verbal reasoning (to detect relative strengths).

◆ The *Lucid Assessment System for Schools* (Horn *et al.*, 1999) is one of the Lucid/CoPS (Cognitive Profiling System) tests that are administered using a computer program and is for children aged 11 to 15 years, 11 months. Its eight tests include an assessment of syllable and phoneme deletions aimed at identifying poor phonological processing ability. An auditory memory sub-test assesses digit span and another sub-test relates to visual memory of objects and spatial position.

◆ The *Special Needs Assessment Portfolio* (*SNAP*) is a computer-aided assessment and profiling kit including a CD-ROM for specific learning difficulties including dyslexia (Weedon and Reid, 2003). It aims to relate the particular pupil's difficulties on to a matrix of learning, behavioural and other difficulties to identify core features including dyslexic, dyspraxic, visual, phonological and attentional difficulties.

Local education authority criteria for the statutory assessment of dyslexia

LEA criteria for the statutory assessment of dyslexia tend to focus on evidence of lower than average attainment in reading, writing or spelling. This does not imply that schools within the LEAs using such criteria do not use approaches taking account of associated difficulties such as phonological difficulties. Rather it means that evidence of dyslexia is taken to be the difficulty in reading, writing and spelling indicated by lower than age average attainment in similar assessment circumstances.

Since 1997, Croydon LEA has used criteria for initiating statutory assessment. These have been developed to link with Early Years Action and Early Years Action Plus. The criteria essentially indicate levels of literacy below which a child would be considered to have a significant difficulty in learning. For example a child aged 7 to 8 years would be considered to be at such a level if he had 'no significant attainment in reading and writing'. For a child of 14 years the level would be a literacy level of 7 years, 6 months (see also Farrell, 2004a, p. 23).

In Blackpool LEA, a panel for statutory assessment moderation advises the Assistant Director (Pupil Support) on whether evidence submitted with a request for statutory assessment of SEN meets locally published criteria. Two of the five criteria developed by the panel are that the school should demonstrate that the pupil's needs are 'exceptional', i.e. significantly greater than other pupils of the same age in the borough; are severe and complex and have highly specialised and long-term implications. The LEA publishes indicators relating to the statutory assessment of specific learning difficulty, which are that three criteria are *all* present. These are:

- a reading age of less than 9 years;
- a reading centile below 20 (that is only 20 per cent of pupils of the same age are likely to have such a low reading level);
- a discrepancy between reading ability and reading level predicted by IQ is at or below the first centile (that is only 1 per cent of pupils of the same age are likely to have such a large discrepancy between their attainment and the attainment predicted by the IQ test).

Guidelines for ceasing a statement of SEN for a pupil with specific learning difficulty indicate that a statement should cease when the pupil has a reading age of 9 years, 6 months or spelling and/or mathematics attainment is above 8 years, 6 months (see also Farrell, 2004b, pp. 23–4).

THINKING POINT

Readers may wish to consider:

- the extent to which the literacy difficulties exemplifying dyslexia can be convincingly related to the supposed underlying features of the condition.

KEY TEXTS

Beaton, A. A. (2004) *Dyslexia, Reading and the Brain: A Sourcebook of Psychological and Biological Research*, London, Psychology Press.

This book gives a lucid, even-handed view of a vast range of research and thinking around dyslexia. In the first part, concerning the 'cognitive context', the author considers difficulties in defining dyslexia; the theoretical context of normal reading development; phonological awareness and phonological recoding; the general language context; and auditory perception, the temporal processing deficit hypothesis and motor skills. In the section on the biological context, the author examines genetic factors; laterality and hormones; neuroanatomical aspects; functional brain imaging and reading; visual aspects of dyslexia; and the magnocellular deficit hypothesis.

Peer, L. and Reid, G. (2003) *Introduction to Dyslexia*, London, David Fulton Publishers.

This short book, published in association with the British Dyslexia Association, discusses the nature of dyslexia, identification and assessment, teaching and learning, helping access to the curriculum with particular reference to learning styles and thinking skills, staff development and resources.

Chapter 3

Dyslexia

Interventions

INTRODUCTION

The sections below first consider interventions predominantly concerning 'associated difficulties' related to dyslexia, that is, interventions for: phonological difficulties; auditory perception difficulties and auditory processing difficulties; visual difficulties and visual processing difficulties; motor co-ordination difficulties; short-term verbal memory difficulties; and sequencing difficulties (relating to sequencing information and chronological events or sequenced activities). I then look at a sample of interventions focusing directly on reading, writing and spelling, although these take into account, to some extent, associated difficulties and other considerations. Other interventions are then examined: developing metacognitive awareness, and identifying and building on strengths (taking account of learning styles and preferred approaches to learning).

Improving sub-skills and compensating for difficulties

Before turning to examples of interventions to do with 'associated difficulties', it may be helpful to set these in context. An important point about the associated difficulties is that they often relate to sub-skills of reading, writing and spelling that need to work together for these activities to be effective. If one or several sub-skills are dysfunctional, then the pupil may find it hard to improve the skill while at the same time having to maintain the other component skills of literacy.

In developing literacy skills, the pupil has to:

◆ process phonological aspects of speech;
◆ process auditory input as part of learning (and where it is weak use other modes to assist);
◆ retain information in short-term memory while it is processed;
◆ use co-ordinated movements for handwriting;
◆ organise information, for example when reading;
◆ sequence information, for example words when reading and letters when writing;

- ◆ orientate letters correctly, for example for writing and spelling;
- ◆ visually focus on words effectively and track words across a written page;
- ◆ auditorily discriminate, sequence, blend and segment sounds in words.

Where these are underpinning or necessary skills, it may be difficult for the pupil to improve one of them while sustaining others. For example, in copying text, the pupil may find it hard to *co-ordinate movements* in handwriting while maintaining the *visual memory* of words just read in order to translate them into handwriting and remember the *sequence* of different letters and words and translate these into written sequences. If the combination of skills makes it hard for the pupil to concentrate on and improve one aspect such as co-ordination then the assumption is that the associated skills (that is, the difficulties associated with them) can be approached distinctively.

For example, if the co-ordinated movements for handwriting are to be taught and improved, the focus on this can be achieved by reducing the demands of the other sub-skills of remembering and translating sequences of different letters from a page of print. The task can involve, for example, the writing of one repeated letter shape related to handwriting. such as the following:

ccccc

oooooo

There is a further assumption attached to remediating activities that a difficulty with a skill may be more general than its particular manifestation in reading, writing and spelling. So difficulty in sequencing letters of the alphabet or letters in words or words in sentences may be associated with other difficulties in sequencing. There may be difficulty sequencing information (e.g. telephone numbers) or chronological events (recalling a sequence of events in a school day, dressing and undressing in the correct order). If this is the case, the assumption is that improving sequencing skills in one sphere will not only remediate important areas of skills such as dressing and knowing the day of the week, but will also carry over to have an indirect effect on sequencing skills necessary for literacy. (This does not necessarily follow, nor does it preclude working directly on the skills relating to literacy at the same time in a simplified form.)

One can see how the indirect effect of skill remediation might apply. For example, in laying out a sequence of items such as coloured bricks from left to right on a table the pupil will be introduced to and encouraged to use positional words such as 'before', 'after', 'next to', 'first', 'last' and so on. This positional understanding and the language linked with it may help the pupil begin to recognise a sequence of letters in a word and be able to talk about their position.

Sometimes, the work related to the associated skills/difficulties includes compensating for any difficulty using resources. For example, a concrete memory aid such as a line of letters of the alphabet taped on the pupil's desk for reference will help with recalling alphabetical order when using a dictionary. The pupil's other abilities are also used in a compensatory way as when a pupil's difficulties with auditory processing and the blending and segmenting of sounds in words is compensated for by multi-sensory methods, including the teaching of phonics using visual and kinaesthetic modes and linking this with word sounds.

It is with such issues in mind that the ensuing section on associated difficulties can be read. As the reader recognises the examples of remediating and compensating for difficulties, he or she will be able to examine and evaluate approaches suggested in other books and other sources that purport to improve the skill and compensate for the difficulty. It is hoped this will lead to a more coherent evaluation of interventions.

Interventions relating to 'associated difficulties'

Interventions relating to phonological difficulties

A pupil with phonological difficulties may be taught to become more aware of, and to use in spoken language, sounds and sequences of sounds that convey meaning in speech. In his own speech, the pupil may practise sounds that he frequently misses, such as word beginnings and endings.

Similarly, speech comprehension practice can be used to help the pupil notice key sounds that convey meaning and changes in meaning. For example, the pupil can be taught to listen for and recognise the sound 's' at the end of a word when it signals a plural as in 'cat' and 'cats'. Speech comprehension can be aided by other sensory modes such as showing accompanying pictures or objects, for example a picture of one 'cat' and a picture of several 'cats'. It would be first established that the difficulty was mainly phonological rather than predominantly grammatical.

To raise phonological awareness, where new vocabulary is introduced, the teacher can encourage pupils' interest in the word or phrase. She will clearly teach and check the pupils' understanding about various aspects of the vocabulary. These aspects include the semantic (word meanings and origins) and grammatical as well as phonological. The phonological aspects may include asking such questions as: How do the sounds of the word break up and blend back together? Do the pupils know any similar sounding words? What are the syllables of the word? (Younger pupils may enjoy clapping them out.) This can be routinely and fairly briefly accomplished for example when key words are introduced at the beginning of a lesson. Such an approach is used effectively in both primary and secondary school and, as well as English teachers, other subject specialists can use the method to reinforce new vocabulary. An approach using interest in speech sounds is 'Metaphon' (Howell and Dean, 1994).

Where the pupil has severe phonological difficulties, a speech therapist will be consulted and may work with the teacher and the SENCO to develop and oversee a suitable programme. (See also the chapter, 'Difficulties with speech', in the book in this series, *The Effective Teacher's Guide to Autism and Communication Difficulties: Practical Strategies.*)

Interventions relating to auditory perception and processing difficulties

Direct teaching and practice of auditory discrimination can be achieved through encouraging the pupil to make progressively finer discriminations in set tasks and exercises such as recognising and discriminating sounds, including letter sounds from an audiotape recording.

Auditory segmenting and blending can be directly taught and practised, for example through playing an audiotape and asking the pupil to listen for certain sounds (such as 'to'). The sounds would be obvious and the pace slow at first, for example 'I am going out **to**morrow'. Auditory blending can be taught using phonics approaches such as those in Phono-graphix™ (www.readamerica.net), which introduces letter sounds and then their blends in teaching reading.

Listening to consonant sounds in different positions can be taught and practised. For example, the pupil would listen for the final consonant in the words, 'dog', 'log' and 'doll' or the initial consonant in 'pit', 'pot' and 'dot' and identify the odd one out.

Multi-sensory teaching and learning may help auditory processing difficulties. If a child with dyslexia finds it more difficult to learn from hearing spoken language, this can be accompanied by information involving other modalities such as visual, kinaesthetic and tactile. This is good practice for all learners but can be particularly helpful for pupils with comparative weaknesses in a particular mode of learning because, first, the preferred mode(s) are likely to be presented and, second, because other modes may reinforce learning in the weaker mode.

For example, visually, charts, diagrams, illustrations, videotapes, Mind Maps™) and spider diagrams can be used to present and record information, while colour can be used for highlighting text. Auditorily, the spoken word can be supplemented by visual aids and gesture. Reading can be complemented by an audiotape recording (as is commonly used in the study of foreign languages) (Crombie and McColl, 2001). Kinaesthetically, role-play, mime and drama can be employed to reinforce learning, while in the tactile mode handling artefacts can assist.

Interventions relating to visual difficulties and visual processing difficulties

It will be remembered that visual difficulties that may be associated with dyslexia relate to convergence, accommodation and tracking.

Convergence involves the eyes converging on the letters of print or handwriting at a distance of about 30 centimetres to ensure that the brain receives a unified picture of the letters and words. Accommodation relates to the skill of being able to quickly adjust the focus of the eyes to changing circumstances, such as the changing distances between print and the eye as the eye moves down a page of writing.

Where visual discrimination is poor, the teacher may use one or more of the many books of activities aimed at encouraging the skill. These may involve several pictures of objects including one that is obviously different and progress to several pictures of objects where the difference is increasingly subtle. The series may be a series of letters with one letter that is obviously different, again progressing to more subtle differences. Practice in visually discriminating letters also involves overlearning one letter, for example 'm', and then introducing a letter with which it is confused, say 'n'. Pupils may be directly taught the different forms of the same letter (upper and lower case).

Using a row of coloured bricks and asking the pupil to separate them into sets of two or three by spacing them may provide practice in visual segmentation. Printed letters of the alphabet can be used to form words and the pupil asked to make segments such as 'b' 'at' or 'su' 'n'.

Tracking concerns the skill of scanning a line of print from word to word and from line to line while 'keeping one's place'. Practice in this skill can be provided by exercises requiring the pupil to give close attention to the text and track it from left to right. For example, the pupil can be asked to track along a sentence or sentences, marking the first letter 'a' then the next letter 'b' then 'c' and so on (e.g. The **a**pple was **b**ig and **c**ol**d** and . . .).

Interventions relating to motor co-ordination difficulties

In handwriting, the early teaching of cursive script can help a pupil having difficulties with fine motor movements. This is because it is more flowing and controllable than forming separate letters and because it enables the pupil to learn handwriting as it were in one go rather than having to learn to write in separate letters then later changing to cursive writing.

Where handwriting includes problems with letter orientation and the reversal of letters (as it does with many pupils who are learning to write), the correct formations may be taught directly. The pupil may begin with large letters, perhaps using a sand tray to emphasise the orientation. The pupil can be encouraged to look at the letter and say the letter as well as tracing it. Later, the pupil will write the letter in a series on paper.

Interventions relating to difficulties in short-term verbal memory

Short-term verbal memory difficulties can be aided by encouraging the pupil to be aware of the settings and conditions he finds conducive to memorising well. These might include actively focusing on the task in hand and not attempting to do something else at the same time, avoiding distractions by using a quiet place and so on. If the pupil has difficulties with short-term verbal memory, instructions are more likely to be remembered if given one at a time.

The embedding of memory (using long-term memory) is facilitated if the pupil is interested and can relate the new information or ideas to what he already knows. These imply the teacher and others working with the child knowing his interests and discussing with him how the new information relates. Material can be learned and remembered better using the multi-sensory approaches already mentioned. It is important that the material to be remembered is well organised and that notes are in order and as necessary divided into more easily manageable sections.

Recall and recognition can be aided by drawing on the sensory modes and particular ways that were used in presenting, recording and studying the information, for example diagrams or mnemonics. Practical strategies to support memory more generally include a diary and computer software that help the pupil to plan workload and homework and other deadlines and provide reminders of these. A substantial part of so-called study skills programmes relate to developing and assisting memory skills.

Interventions relating to sequencing difficulties (temporal order)

Clearly, sequencing is important in speaking, reading, writing and spelling. Sequencing relates to organisation in that aspects of organisation such as dressing, note-taking and many other activities involve following a sequence. As indicated earlier, a pupil may have difficulty sequencing:

◆   information (e.g. letters of the alphabet, telephone numbers);
◆   chronological events and activities (e.g. recalling a sequence of events, knowing the days of the week, dressing in sequence).

Information

Learning sequences such as the letters of the alphabet may be assisted by using a piece of card for each letter and having the pupil place them in front of him in an arc with 'a' on the left and 'z' on the right. The rhythm of learning letters in blocks may help ('a' through 'g', 'h' through 'n', 'o' through 'u', and 'v' through 'z'). It will be seen that handling and laying out the cards uses kinaesthetic memory, speaking the letter sounds and hearing others say them uses auditory memory, and seeing the letters uses visual memory, all helping to establish the sequence (Pollock *et al.*, 2004, pp. 118–19).

Where a dictionary is used, the pages can be marked by post-it notes or a similar device to separate the alphabetical sequence in the same way that the rhythm of the alphabet is divided at 'g', 'n' and 'u', so that the required word is easier to find. Encyclopaedias and other reference books with alphabetically arranged entries could be divided in the same way.

Practice putting information into sequences or finding information already in a sequence can be provided using the principle of beginning with a few items in the sequence and gradually building up. While sequences such as telephone numbers are often simply kept in mobile telephone memories, the pupil will probably wish to memorise his own telephone number, perhaps building up one number at a time.

Where processing sequences of instructions is difficult, the teacher can be careful to make clear requests one part at a time, ensuring that the first request is followed before the second is made. If possible, instructions should be given in the order that they are to be carried out. For example, 'Please finish your calculator work and then hand in your homework' tends to be easier to follow than 'Before you hand in your homework, make sure you finish your calculator work.' Practice in giving and understanding instructions can be gained through role-play in which progressively longer instructions or pieces of information are introduced.

Chronological events, activities and tasks

Sequences such as days of the week may be taught directly using a card for each day of the week. Physically placing on a table the card on which is written 'Monday' and putting next to it (or below it as the pupil prefers) the card for 'Tuesday' and so on gives a visual, kinaesthetic and auditory (as the teacher and the child say the day) framework to aid memory. The days can be linked to pictures of activities associated with the day using the pupil's interests. A similar approach can help with the seasons of the year or the months.

Being able to read the time from an analogue clock involves understanding sequences of numbers and spatial relationships. A principle that can be used is beginning with activities that involve items in relation to the positioning of the pupil's own body. On the floor of the hall or in the school playground a number of cones are placed each bearing a number 1 through 12. The pupil sets these out as a clock face beginning with 12 and then positioning in relation to that the number 6 and then the numbers 3 and 9. The remaining numbers are then put in their relative positions. Once the pupil has a clear memory of the numbers in relation to one another, a smaller scale can be used where the pupil works with a clock face in which there are no numerals and learns to place a series of numerals in their correct position. Learning five minutes past, ten minutes past and so on can be tackled by returning to the hall or playground floor clock and marking these 'times' before working on a smaller card clock with clock hands. The pupil can then 'walk' the large clock to learn minutes *to* the hour such as twenty-five minutes to and twenty minutes to before returning again to the smaller scale. The teacher will need to explain concepts such as 'quarter past' and 'quarter to' to the pupil and provide him with opportunities to practise them.

Sequencing particular activities may pose difficulties and regularly required activities such as dressing and undressing may be directly taught and practised both at home and at school. More time may need to be allowed for activities such as undressing for physical education and dressing again because of difficulties in remembering the sequence in which clothes are put on and taken off.

Interventions for reading

The effectiveness of various intervention schemes was reviewed and evaluated by Brooks (2002). His report, *What Works for Children with Reading Difficulties?*, sought to answer two questions. The first was, 'What intervention schemes are there which have been used in the UK in an attempt to boost the reading, spelling or overall writing attainment of lower achieving pupils in at least one of Years 1–6, and which have been quantitatively evaluated here?' The second question the report sought to answer in relation to intervention schemes was, 'What are those schemes like, and how effective are they?' (p. 1). Among the interventions examined were Phono-graphix™ and 'Reading Intervention', which are considered below to illustrate approaches to reading.

The developers of Phono-graphix™ considered it important to take seriously the fact that English orthography is an alphabet for representing originally and in principle each distinctive speech sound with one symbol. Accordingly, Phono-graphix™ develops the notion that written English is a 'phonemic code' with each sound in a spoken word being represented by some part of a written version. It teaches the phonological skills of blending, segmenting and phoneme manipulation required to use a phonemic code. The approach explicitly teaches correspondences in sound-to-symbol relationships. The so-called 'impact measures' of data on the approach included the largest ratio gain of all the studies reviewed in the Brooks report. One small-scale study involved 12 pupils in an independent specialist school for pupils with dyslexia in Surrey. A 26-week intervention using Phono-graphix™ led to an increase from a pre-test average reading age score on the Macmillan Graded Word Reading test of 6.4 years to a post-intervention average score of 8.7, a ratio gain of 4.5 (www.readamerica.net).

Reading Intervention was formerly called the Cumbria Reading with Phonology Project. It combines phonological training and reading. Pupils are enabled to isolate phonemes within words to come to recognise that sounds can be common between words and that specific sounds can be represented by certain letters. In one study, poor readers in Year 2 were randomly assigned to one of four groups:

1   received systematic training in phonological skills to promote phonological awareness and help in learning to read, similar to the approach used for Reading Recovery;
2   received training in reading only, again on Reading Recovery lines;
3   received teaching in only phonological skills;
4   received normal teaching (the control group).

Experimental groups 1 to 3 received 40 30-minute teaching sessions over a period of 20 weeks. In experimental group 1, the sessions were in three parts. The first part involved reading a familiar book as the teacher made a record of the child's reading so the child could go over familiar words in different contexts. It also encompassed phonological activities and letter identification using a multi-sensory approach of feeling, writing and naming. The second part of the session involved writing a story and cutting it up. The third part of the session introduced a new book. It was found that the reading-only group (group 2) and the phono-logical skills-only group (group 3) made the same sort of progress to the normal teaching control group (group 4). However, the reading plus phonology group (group 1) made significantly better progress in reading than the other three groups (Hatcher, 2000). Brooks (2002, p. 39) states that further research indicates that the initiative continues to be effective for the generality of poor readers, 'and even for children with moderate learning difficulties or dyslexia'.

Among interventions to help reading using multi-sensory methods are talking encyclopaedias. These provide information supplemented by other aids including illustrations and video clips. Encyclopaedias that do not have speech can be accessed through software such as textHELP® that has a read back speech facility, word prediction and other features.

Interventions for writing

Teaching handwriting is also discussed later (see Chapter 4: 'Dyspraxia'), where the focus is on teaching handwriting to children with particular difficulties in motor co-ordination.

In more general terms, letter formation for handwriting may be taught using a cursive script and the teacher can provide a chart to act as a reminder of the shape of each letter. It has been suggested (Pollock et al., 2004) that a well-shaped letter 'c' is a good starting point. The individual letters should be written with an exit stroke so that they can join other letters as follows, cccc. This leads on to teaching the letters, *aa*, *dd*, *gg* and *ee*. These units can then be the initial focus of practice in handwriting exercises even though other letters may be used in general writing. It is suggested that other groups of letters can then be taught. The next group is the letters that determine the writing slant, such as *lll* and *jjj*. Next are the letters that are a combination of curves and angles, such as *bbb* and *fff*. Finally, the letters that can be formed in more than one way can be taught, for example *kk* (Pollock *et al.*, 2004, pp. 109–11).

Another way of improving handwriting is helping the pupil in written work by providing key words and other structures. *Inspiration* is a software package to help the user to develop and organise ideas, using diagrams to help. It allows ideas to be rearranged, which can help with the structure of essays. Templates can be used for different subjects, including science and history. It is published by IANSYST Ltd (see address list). If a pupil is carrying out a piece of extended writing, such as an essay or a research report, actively teaching the skills of how it should be presented is likely to be helpful to all pupils and especially helpful to some pupils with dyslexia. Along with memory-aiding strategies, including organising information and ensuring that it is understood and retained in memory, presentation skills are a central part of study skills programmes. Providing key words likely to be used helps presentation. This enables the pupil to concentrate on what he wants to say without losing time or being unduly distracted by having to mentally or physically (using a dictionary) search for the words he needs. The teacher can provide a structure for the requirements of extended written work for all pupils and this is likely to be particularly helpful for pupils with dyslexia. For example, in a piece of examination course work on sociology, the teacher may provide all pupils with a time plan indicating when the different sections of the work should be handed in for checking. This is supplemented by structured and sequenced requirements for each section. For example, the initial part of the piece of research may require the pupil to set out the hypothesis, the aims of the research and what has been researched by others in the same area. A guidance sheet relating to this would set out examples of what is required.

Note-taking is a further important aspect of writing. Where dictated notes are hindered by poor handwriting, the pupil tends to find it very difficult to concentrate on the content of what is being dictated and simultaneously keep writing legible. The teacher can encourage the pupil to note down key words only. Then at the end of the dictation, a copy of the teacher's notes is given to the pupil who goes through them highlighting the key words he has identified. These act as a revision aid and an anchor for reading the notes.

Word processing programs such as *Microsoft Word* are useful at the different stages of writing a piece of work: planning, composition, checking and correction and publishing (see Blum, 2004, pp. 89–90 for a useful reminder of these processes). Talking word processors allow users to hear, through synthetic speech, the words and sentences they are typing as they are being typed. This can help reassure the pupil that what they are writing makes sense, and, where it does not, allows the pupil to go back and check accuracy. Some programs provide partial or complete sentences to support writing and allow the creation of personalised cloze procedure exercises. Such a program is *Clicker*, produced by Crick Software Ltd (see address list) (www.cricksoft.com).

Interventions for spelling

Pollock *et al.* (2004, pp. 76–84) provide a useful range of approaches to teach spelling, using multi-sensory methods. For example, to teach early letter sounds, it is suggested that the teacher might include the first letter of the child's name, say 'p'. Other letters might be 'm' for 'mum', 't' for 'tiger' and 'a' for apple. These would be taught as the sound that the letter makes rather than the pronunciation of the letter name. For example, 'a' would be 'pronounced as 'a' to rhyme with the sound of the 'a' in 'pan' rather than 'a' to rhyme with the 'a' in 'pane'. The teacher would discuss with the child the sound and the shape of the letter with cards on which the letters are written in front of them. This would lead to basic word-building with words like 'pat' and 'mat' depending on the first few letters that have been introduced.

Early work on visual recall may begin with encouraging the visual recall of objects. This could start with an object to observe in the classroom (e.g. a seashell) that is then covered and the pupils being asked to describe it in as much detail as possible. This would progress to showing words and asking pupils to concentrate on the word to remember as much as they can about it. The teacher prompts with questions such as 'How many letters in the word?' or 'Were any letters the same?' to encourage recall.

The auditory recall of words can be encouraged by games such as clapping out the syllables of the word or grouping words according to their sound, as with 'dog', 'log', 'bog' and so on. Rhymes, poems and songs of course help highlight the sounds of words. As Macintyre and Deponio (2003, p. 67) point out, a child with auditory difficulty may not hear the similarity of words taught in clusters intended to aid spelling ('wish', 'dish'). Therefore the teacher needs to take care that the common rhyme, 'ish', is noticed.

Several approaches use kinaesthetic memory, usually in addition to other sensory modes. For example, in 'simultaneous oral spelling', the pupil says the letters as he writes them so linking kinaesthetic memory and auditory memory.

Among programs useful in developing spelling is *Wordshark* (which can also help with phonic reading). It enables the user to decide how words are grouped and to add words of the user's choice. The program includes games and strategies to help improve spelling. *Wordshark* is produced by White Space Ltd (see address list). *Starspell* employs the 'look, cover, write and check' approach to learning spellings. The words are in 'families' or subject groups but personalised lists can also be made. It is available from Fisher-Marriott (see address list). A spell checker is of course part of the *Microsoft Windows* package.

Other interventions

Developing metacognitive awareness

Strategies that lift to the surface the way one sets about learning and retrieving information can be useful to a pupil with dyslexia, indeed to all pupils. To enable the pupil to apply principles of effective learning that work for him, it is first necessary to help the pupil develop an awareness of learning and thinking – 'thinking about thinking' as it is sometimes called.

The teacher can begin by discussing with the pupil the way that he thinks and learns most effectively and how tasks can be approached in different ways. For example, if the pupil has to learn information for geography homework, how will he gain a meaningful overview of the work first? What essentially is he being asked to do: remember information, comment on it and interpret it? How does the work relate to what the pupil already knows? Is it possible to break the work into more manageable parts without losing meaning? Will diagrams or highlighting help? Where will the pupil study? Will he read silently or aloud? Will he tape himself or someone else reading the information and play it back while he re-reads the text? Will he make notes on what he is reading? How will the information be retrieved? By recalling a series of headings? By using a list or a diagram? (This of course relates to information processing, but the point here is that the pupil is beginning to consider what he normally does, the extent to which it is successful and what other approaches might be suitable.)

Through such discussions, the teacher gains useful information about the pupil's learning strategies and the pupil is encouraged gradually to internalise the critical awareness of thinking and learning that the questions imply and to begin to develop strategies for thinking and learning himself.

Identifying and building on strengths

It is of course important that all pupils, teachers and others are aware of the importance of building the pupil's self-esteem. For pupils with SEN, including pupils with dyslexia, it is particularly important that strengths as well as difficulties are recognised. So it is useful to identify areas of the curriculum and activities in which the pupil can perform well and recognise achievement in these. For example, a pupil with dyslexia may be good at thinking skills (such as problem-solving and decision-making) and, if these are presented without the pupil having to read or write extensively, they can offer areas of success. Open-ended tasks approached through discussion can be used. Such achievements can be used to build the pupil's confidence, motivate the pupil to continue trying in areas they find difficult and act as bridges to support areas of learning difficulty. A pupil who achieves well in art and design might be more motivated to read and write about a favourite artist or painting.

One aspect of building on strengths is taking account of learning styles and preferred approaches to learning. Learning style refers to a person's apparent preferences, skills and abilities to learn in particular ways. This relates to multi-sensory approaches to teaching and learning in that preference for learning in some sensory modes rather than others is considered an aspect of learning style. Another perspective on learning styles is that of the 'inchworm' (analytic) or 'grasshopper' (holistic) styles (e.g. Miles and Miles, 2004). Many pupils will use both approaches but some may have a preference for one approach or the other. This enables the teacher to use the strengths of each strategy and to introduce the pupil to other ways of approaching learning. In practice many lessons will involve the teacher presenting information in both ways, perhaps beginning a lesson with an overview (holistic) and then going on to the steps that exist within it (analytic).

An attempt has been made to relate learning strategies and 'cognitive style' (Riding and Rayner, 1998) in which cognitive style is understood in terms of how affect (feeling), behaviour and cognition are structured and organised. Another approach involves a model of learning styles comprising:

- emotional learning (the need to be motivated by one's interests);
- social learning (the need to be part of a compatible group);
- cognitive learning (the need to know the same as peers);
- physical learning (the need to 'do' and to be active in learning); and
- reflective learning (the need to experiment and explore to discover what facilitates new learning).

(Given, 1998)

A practical way of taking account of a pupil's preferred and most effective approaches to learning is first for the teacher to discuss learning with the pupil and collect observations about his learning preferences. For example, does the child prefer working individually, with one other person or with a small group? Sometimes a task determines the social context in which it is to be taught (teaching conversation as a private individual study session would be somewhat difficult). But often the social aspect of learning can be modified. If a pupil learns better when paired with another pupil with whom he discusses a task, this arrangement can be used as an alternative to private study or group discussion.

THINKING POINTS

Readers may wish to consider:

- how convincing they find the view that, if dyslexia is linked to associated difficulties, working directly on those will improve reading, writing and spelling;
- the extent to which the direct approaches to improving reading, writing and spelling appear to tackle related difficulties;
- how convinced they are by other approaches intended to improve reading, writing and spelling.

KEY TEXT

Pollock, J., Waller, E. and Politt, R. (2004) *Day to Day Dyslexia in the Classroom* (2nd edn), London, RoutledgeFalmer.

As well as looking at the difficulties in reading, spelling and handwriting, this book has chapters on 'speech and language processing', 'movement', 'sequencing' and 'orientation'. In particular, the chapters on handwriting and spelling have some good practical ideas for interventions.

Chapter 4

Dyspraxia

Its nature and interventions

INTRODUCTION

This chapter explores definitions of dyspraxia and its relationship to DCD. I consider the prevalence of dyspraxia and possible causal factors. The chapter examines some associated underpinning processes: gross and fine motor co-ordination and perceptual-motor development (eye–hand co-ordination, visual form constancy, spatial position and spatial relationships). After looking at the identification and assessment of dyspraxia, I outline some of the difficulties experienced regarding handwriting, physical education and personal and social skills and examine various interventions.

Defining dyspraxia

The term 'dyspraxia' is a Greek word meaning difficulty ('dys') with doing or acting ('praxia'). 'Doing' is not simply an act occurring reflexively, but requires conscious thought in organising and directing meaningful action. Dyspraxia may be considered a sub-type of DCD, so it may be helpful to begin with the definition of the latter. Among the diagnostic pointers indicated by the American Psychiatric Association are that DCD is 'a marked impairment of motor co-ordination' that 'significantly interferes with academic achievement or activities of daily living'. The co-ordination difficulties 'are not due to a general medical condition' (American Psychiatric Association, 2000, pp. 56–7).

Focusing more specifically on dyspraxia, definitions tend to emphasise that it is the *organisation* of motor co-ordination that is affected. Dyspraxia is defined in the following terms:

◆ it is an impairment or immaturity of the organisation of movement;
◆ the organisation of thoughts and perceptions are affected;
◆ sometimes the organisation of language is affected;
◆ difficulties are not owing to 'global' learning difficulties but are specific, with most people with dyspraxia having average intelligence;
◆ there are no medically evident neurological signs.

For example, in one definition, it is stated that dyspraxia 'is recognised by a marked impairment in gross and fine motor *organisation* (which may or may not influence articulation and speech) which are influenced by poor perceptual regulation. These difficulties present as an inability to *plan and organise purposeful movement*' (Dixon and Addy, 2004, p. 9, italics in original).

The point about there being no medically evident neurological signs distinguishes dyspraxia from cerebral palsy and other conditions that affect motor co-ordination but in which there are overt neurological symptoms.

A child with dyspraxia has difficulty responding and acting in a timely way when given spoken instructions, when seeing a task demonstrated or when interpreting sensory stimuli (Dixon and Addy, 2004, p. 8). The child 'knows' how to undertake activities but has difficulty organising the movements to accomplish them.

In a similar vein, Cermak *et al.* (2002) define dyspraxia as a difficulty in planning motor acts in the correct sequence. Briefly then, any distinction between dyspraxia and DCD hinges on DCD being seen as a difficulty with co-ordination and execution of movements, while dyspraxia is regarded as a praxis/planning problem. As Kirby and Drew (2003, p. 6) indicate, the child with dyspraxia in this perspective 'does not know what to do and how to move'.

There is a debate about whether the two terms DCD and dyspraxia distinguish very much that would influence decisions about interventions. Kirby and Drew (2003, p. 7) report that, in 2002, at the DCD V International Conference in Banff, Alberta, Canada, there was consensus over using only the term DCD and dropping the expression, 'dyspraxia'.

Developmental verbal dyspraxia (DVD) is a speech difficulty, and as such is considered in another book in this series, *The Effective Teacher's Guide to Autism and Communication Difficulties: Practical Strategies*, in the chapter, 'Difficulties with speech'.

Prevalence

Estimates of the prevalence of dyspraxia in the United Kingdom vary a great deal, one possible interpretation being that identification and assessment are not secure. More boys than girls are identified. Estimates for DCD vary from 6 to 22 per cent, which is thought to depend on the assessment procedure and the background experience of the assessor (Kirby and Drew, 2003, p. 52).

There is often no agreement about who might best assess and there seems to be an assumption that, as well as the child and the parent, several professionals should be involved, perhaps including an occupational therapist, paediatrician, educational psychologist, teacher, physiotherapist, speech and language therapist and SENCO. Perhaps such flexibility is necessary given that some professionals will have more knowledge and experience of dyspraxia than others, but it seems to lead to very varying estimates of when dyspraxia is present, which can do little for the credibility of the identification and assessment.

Possible causal factors

The causes of dyspraxia are not securely known. It is thought that, in some children, the cerebral cortex nerve cells have fewer 'reinforced interconnections'

(Portwood, 1999, p. 10). If neurones in the brain do not form adequate connections, this would suggest that the brain's ability to process information is slowed. If this affects the child's ability to integrate sensory information from different senses, then the development of a body schema for motor planning may be affected. One possible factor is the pre-term delivery of the baby (Padsman *et al.*, 1998).

It has been suggested that fatty acid metabolism may have a role in some neurodevelopmental disorders, including dyspraxia (e.g. Richardson and Ross, 2000). Fatty acids have an important role in myelination, the process relating to the development of myelin, a material formed of fat and protein that forms a protective sheath around some types of nerve fibre. Arachidonic acid and dihomogamma-linolenic acid contribute a fifth of the brain mass and the latter, along with eicosapentaenoic acid, is essential for normal brain functioning. Certain fatty acids cannot be synthesised by the body and must be provided by a person's diet. These are the fatty acids linoleic acid, linolenic acid and arachidonic acid, which are sometimes called the essential fatty acids. These are converted into highly unsaturated fatty acids. A diet with highly processed foods, a lack of fatty fish and deficiency in some minerals such as zinc and in some vitamins can block this conversion. It is thought that some children with neurological disorders may have a difficulty converting the essential fatty acids into highly unsaturated fatty acids because of a problem with either absorption or enzyme deficiency.

Underpinning processes

Gross and fine motor co-ordination

To develop motor control, one must '*understand* the goal, *formulate* a plan and then *execute* the plan' (Dixon and Addy, 2004, p. 14, italics in original). This in turn depends on the child correctly interpreting incoming sensory information from his environment. Three key systems provide information to help develop co-ordinated and controlled movement: the sensory, proprioceptive and vestibular systems. The sensory system perhaps requires no further elaboration in this context, but a little more may be said about the proprioceptive and vestibular systems, in addition to what was covered earlier in Chapter 1.

The proprioceptive system, it will be remembered, provides information about where the limbs are in relation to the body without the need to look. For the child with dyspraxia, this information may not be as acute as for other children, making some activities especially difficult. Dressing can be hard, especially where numerous buttons are involved. Wiping the behind is difficult, with obvious implications for personal hygiene. Riding a bicycle may be problematic without looking at the pedals. Gross motor movement is hard and therefore the child may be heavy footed.

The vestibular system, the reader will recall, involves receptors in the inner ear sending impulses to the brain to assess the position and movement of the head in relation to the rest of the body. This is important for balance and the sense of movement, including velocity. Children in which this system is dysfunctional tend to lack control of the speed of their movements.

Perceptual-motor development

The sensory, proprioceptive and vestibular systems influence visual and auditory perception. Among the interrelated elements of perceptual-motor development affected are eye–hand co-ordination (visual-motor co-ordination); visual form constancy; spatial position; and spatial relationships.

If proprioception, vestibular 'feedback' and the sense of touch are not as acute as is usual, then eye–hand co-ordination is affected. The proprioceptive system gives the incorrect information about where the arm and hand are located (and how much movement is needed to reach an object). Therefore, visuo-spatial judgement is affected, impairing fine motor control.

Visual form constancy involves the ability to recognise that an object that may appear different (for example be in a different position) from when it was first encountered is still the same object. Touch is an important aid to the child developing a mental map of an object and coming to know it as a 'category'. If a child with dyspraxia is getting incorrect information about an object because of a dampened sense of touch, then the important tactile clues about an object are not absorbed. A clear mental schema of the object is not developed and the child may have difficulty developing form constancy, having to rely inordinately on the sense of vision to help.

Developing a notion of one's position in space is an aspect of perception assisting one to appreciate the notion of depth in space; to perceive body position in relation to one's surroundings (e.g. above or below); and to develop a body schema (related to self-awareness) and realistic body image. It helps us develop a notion of body proportions, body symmetry and laterality (the awareness that the body has two distinct sides). Many pupils with dyspraxia have dysfunctional position in space and consequently tend to have poor understanding of self-image, a poor appreciation of body proportions, and a lack of understanding of laterality. Another aspect of body awareness is crossing the midline of the body, which reflects the ability to use the two sides of the body together. A lack of understanding of laterality can lead to difficulties locating left and right and generally poor orientation. The child may avoid crossing the body midline, for example by turning the body so that the left hand can pick up an item on the child's right without the left arm crossing the body midline. The child's writing may be affected; for example, he may produce 'mirror' writing and may reverse letters in words. Map reading will pose great difficulties.

To be said to have an understanding of spatial relationships, a child needs to be able to perceive the position of two or more objects in relation to one another and in relation to himself. Developing this ability depends on developing adequate form constancy, 'position in space' and figure–ground discrimination. Because a pupil with dyspraxia has difficulty in assessing space and judging distances, he will tend to have difficulty in such activities as manoeuvring his way to the front of the class, climbing stairs and especially physical education activities such as walking on benches, climbing wall bars or vaulting. In writing, the size of letters may be very variable and the spacing between letters may be excessive or insufficient. In mathematics, columns for calculations may be inconsistent so that errors are caused and practical tasks involving judging distance will be difficult. More generally, such activities as crossing the road safely will be problematic.

Identification and assessment and some general characteristics of dyspraxia

Identification and assessment

Ideally, several professionals, including a physiotherapist, an occupational therapist, a speech and language therapist where there are language implications, and an educational psychologist conduct the identification and assessment of dyspraxia. For children in the Foundation Stage, the identification of any SEN is a balanced judgement between the possibility of not taking sufficient cognisance of important factors and moving too precipitately to identification. Among assessments are the following.

♦ The *Movement ABC Battery for Children* (Henderson and Sugden, 1992) is for use with children ages 4 to 12 years and includes assessments of ball skills, manual skills and static and dynamic balance. It includes an observational checklist of movement skills in the daily living context. It also has items that assess behaviour problems that might hinder movement performance.

♦ The *Developmental Co-ordination Disorder Questionnaire* (see Crawford *et al.*, 2001) is a parent report assessment to indicate parents' perceptions of their child's skills and, as such, allows the investigation of a child's daily living skills.

A study by Crawford *et al.* (2001), comparing three different tests, found that the assessments did not consistently identify children as having DCD or not having DCD. It was suggested that information from standardised tests along with a view of the child's functional performance may increase the probability that DCD will be identified accurately. Also, observation and assessment based on professional judgement were considered necessary, as well as standardised tests. Identification and assessment draw on identifying as far as possible, underpinning processes or at least their manifestations. They are also informed by recognising as appropriate some of the characteristics outlined in the subsection below.

Some characteristics

Among possible characteristics of dyspraxia at the Foundation Stage are that the pupil has greater than usual difficulties going up or down stairs, learns to use the toilet independently much later than peers, and has difficulty handling toys and games requiring dexterity, such as jigsaws.

The primary school child may find it difficult to use skills in different circumstances because they are not automatic and secure. For example, whereas many pupils will learn to catch a ball of one size and fairly easily adapt to catching a smaller or larger ball, a pupil with dyspraxia may have to almost relearn the skill for the different requirements. The primary school child may be accident prone, tending to knock into objects or knock things over. Older pupils may be disorganised, finding it difficult to move around a large secondary school and to get to lessons on time, especially if there are stairs to negotiate. The pupil may need continuing support to find his way around large secondary school buildings and particularly where buildings are on different sites.

For pupils in primary and secondary school, characteristics of dyspraxia may be evident in various subjects, for example in art, science and design and technology. In some subjects, safety implications such as those involved when handling hazardous substances will necessitate the school making pupil-specific risk assessments. Among other areas in which dyspraxia poses particular challenges are with regard to handwriting; physical activities; and social and personal skills such as eating, using the toilet and dressing.

Handwriting

For pupils of primary school age (5 to 11 years), handwriting may be hindered because of difficulties holding the pencil or positioning letters. Similarly, drawing may be poor because of difficulty with the fine motor movements involved in controlling a pencil. Poor 'position in space' may impair the ability to draw three-dimensional objects. Proportions in drawing may be inconsistent and self-drawings very basic. For pupils of secondary school age (11 to 16+ years), difficulty with writing may be a noticeable feature, as nearly all other pupils will have mastered the skill. At the same time, there are perhaps greater opportunities for a pupil having difficulties forming handwriting and spacing letters to use a word processor routinely. It is important the handwriting is legible and fluent and is produced at speed. In all these aspects, a pupil with dyspraxia may have difficulties. Dixon and Addy (2004, pp. 66–80) make useful suggestions concerning developing handwriting from which the remainder of the section draws.

A child with dyspraxia may adopt a poor writing posture because of proprioceptive difficulties. A better posture is encouraged if the chair and desk height are such that there is a 90° angle between the line of the upper body and the line of the upper leg and between the upper and lower leg at the knee. The positioning of the paper to be written on is important and a pupil with dyspraxia may misjudge this because of spatial difficulties. A sheet of paper should be aligned with the angle of the child's arm and a large card template or other marking on the child's desk will help ensure that this is maintained.

For a pupil with dyspraxia, developing a good pencil grip may be difficult. The grip may be too tight because of poor tactile sensation so that the child feels the pencil better because it is gripped tightly but the fluency and comfort of the writing is affected. Fluency may be further affected because of poor proprioceptive sense in the joints of the fingers and hand. Pencil grip is improved using the pupil's preferred hand and most children have a preferred hand by the age of 7 years, although it may take longer for a child with dyspraxia to develop hand preference than other children. A three-cornered pencil grip or a pen with a rubber finger grip can help. Proprioceptive feedback may be improved by specific tasks aimed at enhancing dexterity.

The pressure of the pencil on the paper may be either too light or too heavy because of proprioceptive difficulties affecting co-ordination and exerting pressure. Physical tasks can be used to temporarily boost upper limb awareness, improvements generally lasting about 40 minutes before further exercises are necessary. For example, one recommended exercise is up to five repetitions of rotating horizontally held arms in small spirals gradually increased, then reversing the direction and reducing the spirals (Addy, 2004). A pen that lights up when pressed for writing can be used to improve a pupil's awareness of pressure on the paper when writing. A pupil who tends to press too lightly will be encouraged to make the pen light up, while a child inclined to press too heavily will be encouraged to avoid illuminating the pen.

A pupil having difficulty with eye–hand co-ordination will find it hard to place the pencil on a particular point, an essential skill for writing. This can be approached obliquely by providing the pupil with opportunities to improve accuracy by tasks such as threading beads or placing pegs in a board. It can be tackled more directly by encouraging increasingly refined movements of the hand and fingers, then of placing a pencil point. For example, the pupil could build confidence and success by placing the finger on a marked area of paper. Gradually the area is decreased so that it is a spot. Next, the pupil will be asked to perform a similar series of tasks but using a pencil, eventually placing the pencil point on a specified dot.

Adequate form constancy is essential because a central part of handwriting involves:

◆ recognising, identifying and distinguishing shapes and different sizes of shapes;
◆ reproducing shapes, correct in form and size.

If the pupil has difficulty with form constancy, multi-sensory approaches may be used to develop the child's experience and understanding of different shapes and sizes. For example, the pupil may sort objects by shape and size or may create shapes using a sand tray or other tactile aid. 'Play-Doh' may be used to make different letter shapes. When a pencil is used, the child begins with making lines and basic shapes, such as a horizontal line, a vertical line, a circle and diagonals. The latter are likely to be particularly difficult for a pupil having problems with laterality because making a diagonal line (\ ) necessitates simultaneously crossing both from left to right and from top to bottom. Spatial copying activities can be used involving a shape to copy written on paper with spaced dots and a similar pattern of dots on which the child draws his copy of the shape.

The child can work on more recognisable pre-writing patterns to help develop the rhythm and fluency necessary for writing. When the child is taught to write letters, their correct shaping may be assisted if lined paper is used with a central line and a line above to indicate the height of an ascending letter and a line below to signify the depth of a descending letter. It is helpful if letters are taught with joins/integral exit strokes to aid the learning of cursive script.

Turning to movement control, the child has to learn the forms of letters and how they join cursively. Because of processing difficulties the child may have difficult stopping a letter and may run the line of a letter on so that, for example, a 'c' has a bottom tail that is far too long. The pupil will need to be taught that the letters have a beginning and an end and some practice writing a series of letters in a specified short line in which the beginning and end is marked by vertical lines can help this.

Because of difficulties with laterality and orientation, pupils with dyspraxia often reverse letters, for example 'b' for 'd' and 'p' for 'q', at an age when most other pupils do not. This can be helped by grouping letters according to whether they are formed by using a clockwise or an anticlockwise motion (Dixon and Addy, 2004, p. 76):

◆ letters formed with a clockwise motion are 'b', 'h', 'j', 'm', 'n', 'p' and 'r';
◆ those shaped using an anticlockwise movement are 'a', 'c', 'd', 'e', 'f', 'o', 'q', 't', 'u', 'v' and 'w';
◆ ones requiring a combination of clockwise and anticlockwise motion are 'g', 's' and 'y'.

Kinaesthetic aids such as the teacher having a pupil write letters in the air and guiding the movements as necessary tend to help the pupil's visual orientation of the letter. Teaching cursive script from an early age tends to help with letter orientation.

Pupils with dyspraxia often space letters and words poorly because of poor spatial organisation. Oblique ways of improving this include making peg-board patterns to help the pupil organise space, and encouraging the pupil to practise tracing a path through maze diagrams. More direct ways of tackling this are introducing cursive writing early and encouraging the pupil to leave a finger space between words, although this works better with pencil writing than writing with a pen where it is easy to smudge work.

Fluency in writing is difficult for a child with dyspraxia to attain. Moving from pre-writing patterns to the formation of letters with joins/integral exit strokes to cursive writing can assist the fluency of the pupil. That is, writing 'separate' printed letters is not taught. A kinaesthetic approach, for example using a sand tray or chalk board for writing letters, helps the child develop a mental image of the letter forms and how they link together. Commercial writing programs are also used, such as *Handwriting Without Tears*™ (Olsen, 2000), which is published by Harcourt Assessment (see address list).

A school may consider that a pupil's writing difficulties will hinder perform-ance in an examination to such an extent that the pupil will not be able to demonstrate fairly what he knows and can do. If so, the school may apply to the examination board for special arrangements to be made, such as allowing the pupil extra time, the use of a word processor or a scribe.

Physical education

The importance of offering some success in physical activities is indicated in the observations of Bundy (2002). She suggests a child with DCD may be seen to be participating in activities and games with other children but may not be getting as much enjoyment as others. Also, as children with DCD are likely to be less competent, they may be less accepted by peers, which can lead to isolation and feelings of low self-worth.

For a pupil with dyspraxia, physical activities in general pose a challenge. Skipping with or without a rope may be difficult. Riding a bicycle is a complex physical task in any event, involving balance, co-ordination and constantly processing and responding to visual information for steering. For a child with dyspraxia, having difficulties in co-ordination, spatial difficulties and poor judgement of speed, it is hardly surprising the skill in learning to ride a bicycle is delayed. In physical education, spatial difficulties will make it hard for the child to move about among apparatus. Difficulties judging distance and velocity will make many ball games very challenging. In the case of secondary-aged pupils some co-ordination difficulties may be less noticeable, as many pupils will be going through a clumsy period because of the adolescent growth spurt.

At Key Stage 1 of the National Curriculum for physical education, regarding knowledge and understanding, teaching is intended to ensure that pupils are 'acquiring and developing skills', 'selecting and applying skills, tactics and compositional ideas', 'evaluating and improving performance' and developing 'knowledge and understanding of fitness and health'. The breadth of study includes dance activities, games activities and gymnastic activities (DfEE/QCA, 1999a, pp. 130–1). At Key Stage 2 further development is encouraged in knowledge and understanding. The breadth of study is extended to include two activity areas from 'swimming activities and water safety', 'athletic activities' and 'outdoor and adventurous activities' (pp. 132–3). At Key Stages 3 and 4, knowledge and understanding and activity participation are further developed. For a pupil with difficulties in fine and gross motor co-ordination, poor proprioception and other difficulties, physical education presents a real challenge.

A pupil with dyspraxia may be seen by a physiotherapist outside school time, but there is scope for innovative work when a teacher teaching physical education and a physiotherapist work together preparing and implementing PE lessons in which pupils with dyspraxia are included. Programmes have been devised that seek to meet the requirements of the National Curriculum and also enable pupils with dyspraxia to participate fully in activities that help their particular difficulties. For example, a carefully structured ten-lesson programme has been developed and implemented that covers a half term of two 45-minute sessions per week. It aims to develop motor co-ordination within the school curriculum for pupils in the latter part of Key Stage 1 and can be adapted to suit pupils in the earlier parts of Key Stage 2 (Dixon and Addy, 2004, pp. 102–12). To illustrate, lesson 1 includes such activities as placing two rows of mats along the floor and following the leader to crawl across the room on the mats; having a high-knee walking race; and playing a game of 'crawling football' (pp. 102–3).

It is important that activities are framed so that all pupils can participate in PE lessons. Black and Haskins (1996) have suggested ways in which activities can be structured to achieve this: parallel activity; inclusive adapted activity; and discrete adapted activity. These are illustrated below using the example of ball skills.

In a *parallel activity*, pupils play a game together but in their own way so that they use different strategies to reach for the same goal. For example, if the aim is to improve skills in being able to 'send and receive a ball' (DfEE/QCA, 1999a,

p. 131, section 7a), then pairs of pupils who have acquired this skill can pass the ball while moving and from several yards apart while others who are still developing the skill can pass while standing still and closer to each other. An *inclusive adapted activity* is one in which the games and activities are adapted so that all pupils can take part. For example, for older pupils, a game of volleyball can be adapted using a lighter ball such as a sponge ball so that there is more time for pupils who do not have advanced skills in relation to the game to position themselves and reach the ball. Pupils who are skilled at the game will tend to enjoy such adaptations from time to time because the timing of the skills is changed and there is a different element of challenge. In a *discrete adapted activity*, pupils take part in pairs or practise individually. For example, in practising a skill for a game in which a bat is used to strike a ball (e.g. rounders), a pupil with dyspraxia may practise using a larger bat or a lighter ball.

In general, a pupil with dyspraxia may find the PE lesson daunting. Having a space for each child to which they return, for example in gymnastics, can help provide a sense of predictability and security that is reassuring. Also, markings on the floor to indicate the paths that pupils are expected to follow will help the child with dyspraxia with orientation and direction.

For a pupil with dyspraxia, changing for PE and changing back to day clothes afterwards in the limited time usually allowed is difficult. Clothing adapted using false buttons and Velcro fasteners can help this.

Making physical education and activities motivating and enjoyable for pupils with dyspraxia, while it is undoubtedly important, poses a challenge for teachers. In a study comparing the responses of 81 adolescents with 'motor learning difficulties' with those of peers without such difficulties, similar attitudes to the benefits of physical activity were found. However, adolescents with motor learning difficulties were involved in far fewer physical activities than peers (Larkin and Parker, 1999).

Personal, social, health and citizenship education (PSHCE)

Pupils with dyspraxia can become frustrated and demoralised and come to feel of low self-worth because of the persistent difficulties they face that may not always be understood by others. Such feelings may express themselves at times in difficult behaviour. In such circumstances the teacher and others will try to understand the root cause of the behaviour. The greater the extent to which the teacher and others can develop understanding of dyspraxia and the greater their skills in supporting a pupil with dyspraxia, the greater the likelihood that the pupil will be able to deal with the changes of education and other day-to-day demands.

Within the area of PSHCE, the aspects of personal and social skills pose particular difficulties for pupils with dyspraxia. Several difficulties influence the development of social skills. Motor-perceptual difficulties can make it difficult for the child or young person to realise that they may have the proximity wrong when speaking to another person, for example by standing too close. Because of spatial and orientation difficulties, the child may have a poor appreciation of his own body language and be insufficiently aware of the importance and subtlety of gesture and body position. Gesture may not be well co-ordinated with speech. Related to this, he may not be aware of the signals from other people conveyed by non-verbal communication and may miss clues that aid smooth interaction.

Poor co-ordination may inhibit participation in social activities such as dancing, ice-skating and ten-pin bowling. Using public transport and finding one's way after asking directions may be hindered by orientation difficulties. Handling small coins can be problematic, particularly if one is under time pressure as when at the front of a shop queue.

Regarding eating, the primary school pupil with dyspraxia may have difficulty co-ordinating a knife and fork, may spill liquids and may take a long time to finish eating a meal. In preparing a meal, activities such as using a can opener and buttering bread may be tricky. A wall can-opener and cutlery with thick rubber handles are possible adaptations.

Moving about in a way that does not involve bumping into people or knocking into or knocking over objects may be difficult in itself. Co-ordination difficulties hinder involvement in team games requiring high levels of motor co-ordination, such as football, some computer games and board games.

Social skills can be taught using established behavioural techniques, such as modelling and the positive reinforcement of behaviours approaching what is desired. Another approach is role-play, perhaps following an adult modelling required behaviour, such as standing a sufficient distance from someone one does not know well when speaking.

After-school social skills sessions for groups of pupils with dyspraxia have been developed and used to positive effect (Dixon and Addy, 2004, pp. 126–37). These include, for example, activities to encourage higher self-esteem. In a session to promote more effective non-verbal communication, one activity is that each member of the group, given a different card describing an emotion such as 'frightened' or 'happy', tried to convey that emotion non-verbally (p. 129). In another session on spatial awareness and personal space, one activity involved a blindfolded member of the group standing in the middle of the room while others tried to sneak across the room without being caught (choosing a suitable path, being aware of space and distance from the blindfolded person). After each session, homework is given to reinforce, develop and apply what is learned.

Both personal hygiene and personal appearance can influence social acceptance by peers. For primary school pupils, using the toilet may be problematic because wiping the bottom involves spatial and proprioceptive skills as the part of the body concerned is out of view. Also, for girls, unless the technique of wiping the bottom with a movement towards the back is learned, there is a risk of urinary infection. False buttons above Velcro fasteners on clothing and trousers with an elasticised waist can save time dressing and undressing for the toilet – an important factor if the child wishes to use the toilet in the allocated break times without being late for lessons. Wet wipes rather than hard toilet paper can clean the bottom more thoroughly and easily. A small foot rest by the toilet can be useful for all younger pupils so that the legs are not dangling down and the child does not have to grasp the side of the toilet to keep balance. A child with dyspraxia will find this particularly helpful. A mirror behind the door of at least one toilet cubicle will allow the child with dyspraxia to see himself when dressed and check that he is tidy. At secondary school age, hygiene may still be problematic. Girls may find changing sanitary products very difficult.

Dressing may pose problems for primary-aged pupils because of poor co-ordination, impaired body image, poor proprioceptive feedback (for parts of garments that cannot be seen while dressing) and poor laterality. This tends to lead to difficulties fastening and unfastening buttons and hooks and dressing where the body part cannot be seen. Changing for physical education lessons in limited time will be challenging. Older secondary-aged pupils may still be dishevelled in their appearance and girls may find it problematic to apply make-up sparingly.

THINKING POINTS

Readers may wish to consider with reference to a particular school or schools:

◆   what training has taken place for staff regarding dyspraxia;
◆   how effectively dyspraxia is identified and assessed in local schools;
◆   the range of interventions with which staff feel confident;
◆   the extent to which interventions tackle associated/underlying difficulties and overt manifestations of dyspraxia.

KEY TEXTS

Dixon, G. and Addy, L. M. (2004) *Making Inclusion Work for Children with Dyspraxia: Practical Strategies for Teachers*, London, RoutledgeFalmer.

This is at times an impassioned book seeking to convey the impact of dyspraxia on the child and his family as well as providing suggestions for activities and approaches for use by teachers and others.

Kirby, A. and Drew, S. (2003) *Guide to Dyspraxia and Developmental Co-ordination Disorders*, London, David Fulton Publishers.

Particularly useful in this book are various tables indicating developmental expectations in different areas, such as 'the development of body perception in children' and 'the development of handwriting skills in children'.

Chapter 5

Dyscalculia
Its nature and interventions

INTRODUCTION

This chapter defines dyscalculia and some characteristic difficulties, and outlines some of the different types that have been suggested. I look briefly at causal factors and at the identification and assessment of dyscalculia, and comment on the difficulty of estimating its prevalence. The chapter explains the prerequisite skills needed to form a basis for mathematics understanding and how the teacher can help the pupil develop them. I explain some further interventions appropriate for pupils with dyscalculia. The chapter then examines mathematics difficulties associated with dyspraxia and with dyslexia.

Definition

Dyscalculia is a difficulty in understanding and learning mathematics that is not associated with general learning difficulties such as moderate, severe or profound learning difficulties and is therefore considered to be a specific learning difficulty. It has been described as follows.

> Dyscalculia is a condition that affects the ability to acquire mathematical skills. Dyscalculic learners may have difficulty understanding simple number concepts, lack an intuitive grasp of numbers, and have problems with learning number facts and procedures. Even if they produce the correct answer or use the correct method, they may do so mechanically and without confidence.
>
> (DfES, 2001c)

Among characteristic difficulties of dyscalculia are that the pupil may have difficulty performing simple calculations such as addition; have difficulty knowing how to respond to mathematical information; substitute one number for another; invert numbers (e.g. 6 for 9); reverse numbers (e.g. 2 for 5); misalign symbols, for example when using a decimal point; and name, read and write mathematical symbols incorrectly.

Attempts have been made to identify and delineate different 'types' of dyscalculia and these extend and supplement basic definitions:

- *Spatial dyscalculia* relates to difficulties in visuo-spatial assessment and organisation.
- *Anarithmetria* involves confusion with arithmetical procedures, for example mixing written operations such as addition, subtraction and multiplication.
- *Lexical dyscalculia* (alexia) concerns confusion with the language of mathematics and its relationship with symbols (e.g. subtract, take away, deduct, minus and '−').
- *Graphic dyscalculia* (agraphia) refers to problems with being able to write the symbols and digits needed for calculations.
- *Practographic dyscalculia* concerns impairment in the ability to manipulate concrete objects or graphically illustrated objects. The child has difficulty in practically applying mathematical knowledge and procedures. A child may be unable to arrange objects in order of size, compare two items according to size, or state when two items are identical in size and weight (Senzer, 2001).

It will be apparent that some of these supposed types of dyscalculia appear to be related to either dyslexia or dyspraxia. For example, spatial dyscalculia may relate to dyspraxic difficulties, while lexical and perhaps graphic dyscalculia may relate more to dyslexic difficulties.

Causal factors

Foetal alcohol syndrome has been associated with babies being born with the parietal lobes being underdeveloped. (The parietal lobes are surface regions of the brain hemispheres named after the overlying parietal bones of the skull.) The parietal lobes are considered important for numeracy, and underdevelopment is associated with the child later having difficulties with mathematical cognition and number processing (Kopera-Frye *et al.*, 1996).

Different neural systems contribute to mathematical cognition, one of which is a verbal system (Dehaene *et al.*, 1999). This appears to store, as well as verbally rote-learned information such as poetry, number facts such as number bonds, and underpins counting and numerical rote-learned knowledge like multiplication tables. If a child with dyscalculia also has dyslexia, and if dyslexia has a phonological basis, then it may be that the neural system affected will be the verbal system that underpins counting and calculation (Goswami, 2004, p. 179).

Another neural system concerned with the representation of number appears to underpin knowledge concerning numbers and their relations (for example one number being larger or smaller than another) (Dehaene *et al.*, 1998). Located in the intraparietal areas of the brain, the system is activated by such tasks as number comparisons (whether using numerals, words or clusters of dots).

Visuo-spatial regions may be involved with complex calculations (Zago *et al.*, 2001) where visual-mental imagery may be important. A particular parietal-premotor area is activated during finger counting and calculation (Goswami, 2004, p. 179).

Identification and assessment

In identifying dyscalculia, the teacher will bear in mind the definition of dyscalculia and its possible characteristic difficulties. The identification and assessment of dyscalculia is also informed by other difficulties a pupil may have. For example, if the pupil is identified as having dyslexia, then mathematics difficulties are assessed within that context. Similarly, should a child be considered to have dyspraxia, mathematics difficulties would be assessed in that light. Among commercial assessments is the computer-based *Dyscalculia Screener* (Butterworth, 2004), which measures pupils' response times and the accuracy of the responses and is intended for children aged 6 to 14 years.

Prevalence

It is difficult to estimate the prevalence of dyscalculia because it is not always regarded as a separate 'condition'. General observations can be made about mathematical difficulties and related interventions are developed from these. However, often, mathematics difficulties are associated with dyslexia and with dyspraxia and interventions are developed within that context.

'Prerequisite skills' and how they can be taught

There are certain basic prerequisite skills necessary in mathematics. If these are not securely in place, then the child will have difficulty developing subsequent skills and understanding. Certain prerequisites are implied in work at the Foundation Stage. At that stage, 'early learning goals' provide that a pupil's early experience of mathematics includes:

- counting and using numbers to at least 10 in familiar contexts;
- recognising numerals 1 to 9;
- talking about and creating simple patterns;
- beginning to understand addition as combining two groups of objects and subtraction as 'taking away';
- describing the shape and size of solid and flat shapes;
- using everyday words to describe position;
- using early mathematical ideas to solve practical problems.

(DfEE/QCA, 1999a, p. 62)

Prerequisite skills for mathematics can also be understood in terms of classification, number, length, area, volume, weight, position and movement, each of which will now be examined in turn.

Classification

At Key Stage 1 (ages 5 to 7 years) pupils should be taught to 'solve a relevant problem by using simple lists, tables and charts to sort, classify and organise information' (DfEE/QCA, 1999a, p. 64 [Ma2, 5a]). Classification begins with very simple distinctions such as 'same' and 'different' and extends to more sophisticated classifications such as grouping shapes with the same number of sides and angles.

A pupil who has difficulty recognising patterns of relationships and problems recognising groups (such as groups of objects of the same colour) will have difficulty in classifying. Practical experience of and practice in classifying will help. The teacher will begin with easy classifications and make them gradually more complex.

Number

In the National Curriculum, during Key Stage 1 pupils 'learn to count, read, write and order numbers to 100 and beyond' (DfEE/QCA, 1999a, p. 62). Underpinning the development of the understanding of number in the Foundation Stage and Key Stage 1 are various elements that need to be understood. If a pupil is having difficulty with number, it is helpful to check that the following precursors are in place and to teach them if they are not.

The pupil may have difficulty with concepts relating to 'more' and 'less'. He may have difficulty learning that one number has a greater value than another (e.g. 5 and 3). There may be a difficulty relating size to quantity, for example knowing that five tiles laid out on a flat surface will take up a smaller space than will ten tiles of the same size laid out in a similar way. The pupil may have difficulty in estimating an answer before working it out. He may confuse the direction in which things get bigger or smaller. One source of this confusion may be that in a number line (1, 2, 3 . . .), numbers to the left are progressively smaller in value, but with digits the value to the left is bigger in the sense that it represents tens, hundreds, etc. (e.g. in '24' the '2' at the left represents '20') (see Poustie, 2001b, p. 7).

A pupil may have particular difficulties with place value. These may relate to numbers being misread, so that the correct information is not used; numbers being miswritten, in which case the pupil may know the correct answer to a calculation but miswrites it; and not understanding the concept, for example because of difficulties in understanding the language used. In order to remedy any mistakes relating to place value, it is important for the teacher to ask the pupil to explain his working out so the correct remediating strategy can be determined.

Length

At Key Stage 1 of the National Curriculum, pupils should be taught to 'compare and measure objects using uniform, non standard units, then with a standard unit of length (cm, m)' (DfEE/QCA, 1999a, p. 66 [Ma 3, 4a]). Also, pupils should be taught to 'estimate, measure and weigh objects' (p. 66 [Ma 3, 4c]).

A precursor to understanding length, such as the length of a line, is grasping that length is 'conserved' even when the line is bent or curved. A pupil who has difficulty with this notion would be shown two straight pieces of wire and recognise that they were the same length. If one of the pieces of wire was then bent into, say, an 'S' shape, the pupil would not recognise or accept that it was still the same length as its partner. The misunderstanding may relate to assuming that length has to do with the length of the space that the wire occupies (which is smaller when the wire is bent) rather than it being a retained property of the wire. One way of helping with this difficulty is through the teacher providing plenty of experience that length stays the same by very gradually bending the wire and having the pupil agree that it is the same length as before, then progressively bending it a little more.

Area

In Key Stage 2 of the National Curriculum (ages 8 to 11), pupils should be taught to 'find areas of rectangles using the formula' (DfEE/QCA, 1999a, p. 72 [Ma3, 4e]). Among the prerequisite skills required for understanding area is the ability to match circumscribed areas, for example the pupil should be able to match two squares of identical areas from several squares with different areas. This can be taught directly, giving the pupil plenty of experience of matching area visually. To begin with the pupil can be given a square and a choice of two other squares only one of which matches the pupil's square. Later the number of squares can be increased. Later still the pupil can be asked to match two squares from several that are laid out on the table, so that the pupil has to identify both squares.

Volume

At Key Stage 1, pupils should be taught to 'compare and measure objects using uniform and non-standard units, then with a standard unit of length (cm, m), weight (kg), capacity (l)' (DfEE/QCA, 1999a, p. 66 [Ma 3, 4a]). At Key Stage 2, pupils should be taught to 'recognise the need for standard units of length, mass and capacity' (p. 72 [Ma 3, 4a]). A prerequisite skill in understanding volume is that the pupil realises that volume is 'conserved' even if the container of the substance is different in size and/or shape. A pupil who has difficulty with this should be given plenty of practical experience using liquids and containers of different sizes and shapes, care being taken not to spill the liquid so that it can be demonstrated that the volume of liquid remains the same.

Weight

At Key Stage 1 of the National Curriculum, pupils should be taught to 'compare and measure objects using uniform, non standard units, then with a standard unit of length (cm, m), weight (kg), capacity (l)' (DfEE/QCA, 1999a, p. 66 [Ma 3, 4a]). Also, pupils should be taught to 'estimate, measure and weigh objects' (p. 66 [Ma 3, 4c]). In Stage 2 pupils should be taught to 'recognise the need for standard units of . . . mass' (p. 72 [Ma3, 4a]).

Among precursors to understanding weight is that the pupil grasps the 'conservation' of weight. This implies that the pupil will understand that, if two malleable items weigh the same and one of the items is made into a different shape, it will still weigh the same as the other item. A useful suggestion for teaching this is beginning with the pupil's own body weight. The pupil would check his weight on scales then check it when he was standing or crouching to show that the weight is constant. This then develops into weighing items and changing their shape and then weighing them again to confirm that the weight is the same (Poustie, 2001b, pp. 22–3).

Position and movement

At Key Stage 1 of the National Curriculum (ages 5 to 7), pupils should be taught to 'observe, visualise and describe positions, directions and movements using common words (DfEE/QCA, 1999a, p. 65 [Ma 3, 3a]). Also, pupils should be taught to 'recognise movements in a straight line (translations) and rotations, and combine them in simple ways' (p. 65 [Ma 3, 3b]). In Key Stage 2 (ages 8 to 11), pupils should be taught to 'transform objects in practical situations, transform images using ICT' and 'visualise and predict the position of a shape following a rotation, reflection or translation'. They should be taught to 'identify and draw 2-D shapes in different orientations on grids' and 'locate and draw shapes using co-ordinates in the first quadrant, then in all four quadrants' (pp. 71–2 [Ma3, 3a, 3b, 3c]).

For a pupil with difficulties in these aspects of position and movement, early work can involve the pupil developing an understanding of his own position in relation to other objects beginning with simple tasks and single objects. The pupil might, for example, be asked (and if necessary guided) to stand in front of a box, beside a box, behind a box and so on. The pupil would later direct another person into similar positions to give the pupil practice in using the correct expressive vocabulary.

General interventions

General features of good teaching, as well as some more specific interventions, help pupils with dyscalculia. Attention problems may include difficulties in attending to each element of a calculation. The pupil may have difficulties following the teacher's explanations of calculations. The pupil may find it hard to check his work with much reliability. Sometimes difficulties with attention are created or exacerbated by stress or anxiety about doing mathematics. It is important for the teacher when teaching a class or group to ensure that the pupil is giving attention, for example by using the pupil's name. If explanations are broken into small steps, attention may be assisted as long as the purpose and context of the steps are clear to the pupil. Reassuring the pupil and trying to make mathematics learning enjoyable perhaps through using games can help reduce anxiety and help the pupil relax and therefore concentrate and attend better. Where anxiety about mathematics is high, individual tuition can help ensure early success and reduce the anxiety of not getting the task right.

The pupil may experience difficulty in adapting existing knowledge, finding it hard to dispense with procedures that are not suited to the task in hand. For example, physically adding to 6 existing items different numbers of items (e.g. 2, 3, 4), the pupil may count from one every time instead of adapting the counting approach and counting on from 6.

Regarding generalising mathematical skills, the pupil may learn an approach in one situation with one set of items but not apply it in another situation with other items when most other children would do so. In general, plenty of practice and application in different contexts will help embed mathematical concepts and terms.

The pupil may find it difficult to apply mathematical learning such as being able to count money to practical situations like spending money in a shop.

Structured teaching of different strategies and practice in using them can help with adapting knowledge. Similarly, the pupil may be taught to apply approaches and skills to different situations. Applying knowledge can be helped if the teacher ensures that the skills are very secure then gradually introduces the extra demands of applying the knowledge and skill in different circumstances. For example, using money in shopping can begin with buying a single item with a known price using the exact amount of money. This will allow the pupil to cope better with the social demands of the shopping. Later the task can be made increasingly more complicated, for example requiring change.

Among important aspects is that whenever possible the teacher makes the work *relevant* and meaningful. Time explaining why some aspect of mathematics needs to be learned and how it can be used is time well spent. Links to the pupil's interests and hobbies are motivating.

A careful judgement is needed when breaking tasks into small steps to try to aid understanding. If the overall picture is not understood, such small steps can seem disparate and therefore be harder to remember. So, for example, if the teacher is explaining the steps in a division calculation, the idea of dividing and why it is necessary will be reviewed before the steps are followed, so that it is clearer where the steps are leading. This is a specific example of the more general strategy of bringing together an overview of a task and the step-by-step approach to it.

The use of concrete apparatus helps give the pupil experience and understanding of what is being done. A pupil with dyscalculia may require consolidation using concrete items for longer than most pupils. Once more abstract methods are being used concrete reminders can still be helpful for some tasks. These might include number lines, a box of physical shapes that are labelled and so on. Cuisenaire rods, designed by Gattegno in the 1950s, are useful physical aids using size and colour to help pupils' understanding of many aspects of mathematics (see Poustie, 2001b, pp. 61–3 for further ideas). Westwood (2000) accepts that structural apparatus 'provides a bridge between concrete experience and abstract reasoning by taking learners through experiences at intermediate levels of semi-concrete . . . to the semi-abstract' (p. 41). But he gives a timely reminder that such apparatus is by no means foolproof in helping pupils acquire understanding. For example, the pupil may not connect the activities carried out using the apparatus to the mathematical concepts that the teacher wishes to convey. The teacher still needs to discuss with the pupil the task and assess the child's understanding.

Multi-sensory approaches where in particular the visual, auditory and kinaesthetic senses are used can help learning. For example, where a pupil has a preferred sensory mode for learning, it will help to ensure that that mode is one of the sensory modes stimulated by the teaching. ICT software such as *Numbershark*, published by White Space Ltd (see address list), can help stimulate the pupil by presenting him with a structured program on which the pupil can work and progress in his own time. Sound, vision and movement are all used.

Mathematics and dyspraxia

Bearing in mind the underlying difficulties associated with dyspraxia and some of the approaches suggested in relation to handwriting, it is possible to understand why certain difficulties arise in mathematics and how they might be tackled. The following approaches are therefore illustrative rather than exhaustive.

Number

Because of such difficulties as those with fine motor co-ordination, eye–hand co-ordination and spatial relationships, the child with dyspraxia may have difficulties with writing numerals, for example getting the correct size. Squared paper with squares of a size that allow the child to write a number in each can be used to help with the size of numerals.

The orientation of numerals may be problematic, for example the pupil may write '2' for '5' or '6' for '9'. This can be helped by kinaesthetic approaches, writing the numeral in a sand tray or other tactile medium. It has also been suggested that numerals can be taught in groups that avoid the teaching of very similar numerals that may be confused (3 and 5; 6 and 9). The groups would be introduced as 1, 2 and 3 with particular care that 3 was formed and practised before 5 was introduced. Next 4, 5 and 6 would be taught with care that 6 is practised before 9 is taught. The next group would be 7, 8, 9 and 10 (El-Nagar, 1996).

Spacing between numerals may be excessive or insufficient just as it may be in the writing of alphabetic letters. Columns for calculations may be inconsistent so that errors are made. Using squared paper may help both of these.

Difficulties with orientation may make it difficult for the pupil to follow and reproduce the sequence of a calculation from left to right or from top to bottom. This will need to be carefully and explicitly taught and the pupil can be reminded of the direction of the calculation by the use of arrows written in a different colour to that used for the child's calculations at the beginning of a horizontal calculation and at the side of a top to bottom calculation, as indicated below:

$$\rightarrow 6 + 7 = 11 \qquad \begin{array}{r} 6\ + \\ 7 \\ \hline \\ \hline \end{array} \downarrow$$

Because of such difficulties as those with laterality, the pupil may have problems recognising and understanding mathematical symbols like '=' and '÷'. He may also confuse symbols that look similar but have a different orientation, such as '+' and '×'.

Also, difficulties with motor co-ordination may lead to a symbol being incorrectly written or copied, for example '+' for '×'. If therefore a pupil writes '5 + 2 = 10' this may reflect an incorrect calculation or it may indicate that the pupil was attempting to write '5 × 2 = 10'. As with all pupils, it is important to ask the pupil to explain the working out so that such misunderstandings come to light.

Such difficulties with symbols can be helped by using multi-sensory approaches, particularly visual, auditory, kinaesthetic and tactile methods, perhaps using a sand tray to practise writing the symbols that are also spoken and heard. Numerous games and activities can be used to reinforce the recognition of symbols, such as adapted versions of lotto, dominoes and Pelmanism.

If the pupil has difficulties with the fine motor movements necessary to operate a calculator accurately, a large-key calculator can be used.

Shape, space and measure

Because of such difficulties as orientation, the pupil with dyspraxia may have problems understanding and using positional words and phrases such as 'up' and 'down', 'behind' and 'in front', and linking them to different aspects of spatial relationships. These words will need to be explicitly taught and linked with practical experience of the positions they convey. The teacher may begin by applying the words to the position of the pupil's own body, for example teaching the pupil positions such as standing 'behind' a tree and standing 'in front' of the tree. The task can then move to developing understanding of the position using models (in this case of a figure representing the pupil and a model representing the tree) and having the pupil manipulate these to develop and confirm understanding. The pupil may then be taught the position using two-dimensional representations such as immediately observable digital photographs (of himself standing behind a tree) and drawings.

Regarding shape, the pupil having difficulties with form constancy may not see shapes accurately and when required to reproduce them from memory will have difficulties doing so both in terms of form and size. This will be exacerbated when the pupil has difficulties with fine motor co-ordination that will make it hard for him to draw a shape even if he had visualised it accurately. Difficulties with laterality will tend to make it difficult for the pupil to draw shapes involving diagonals where the lines involve negotiating two sets of directions: left–right and up–down.

Recognising shapes can be helped in various ways. The teacher can encourage the pupil to handle and explore physical shapes such as a square or a triangle. Also helpful is the use of multi-sensory approaches, especially kinaesthetic and tactile methods, to encourage the accurate reproduction of shapes. For example, shapes can be drawn in a sand tray or made from plasticine.

Also concerning shape, the child may struggle to understand symmetry because of problems identifying left and right. This can be taught through games in which the child's own body is the first indicator of what is left and right (not the teacher's left and right as she faces him). With his own left hand and right hand marked and facing an agreed way, the child is asked to go to his left or to his right. With a group, 'Simon says' can be a vehicle for introducing and practising this in an enjoyable way. Later, looking at a shape that can be physically handled and which has a clear line of symmetry, the pupil will be asked to show the left and the right of the shape. Drawings of shapes can then be used to check the pupil's understanding of the concept and to teach and reinforce it further.

The pupil may have particular difficulty in recognising three-dimensional shapes and drawings of such shapes and trying to draw a three-dimensional shape will be particularly hard. The teacher can provide plenty of guided opportunities for the pupil to handle and talk about three-dimensional shapes. A carefully structured programme in which the pupil is introduced to two-dimensional representations of simple three-dimensional shapes with the latter present can help the pupil begin to match and recognise the aspects of the three-dimensional shape and the representation.

Turning to weight, pupils with poor proprioception, whose muscle receptors are not as sensitised as those of most other children, have difficulty with understanding weight. A general approach that is useful is to provide the pupil with plenty of structured experience of handling objects of different weights. Terms such as 'heavy', 'light', 'lighter than' and 'heavier than' need to be learned and understood. The pupil is introduced to measuring weight using a balance where the respective relative weights of items are indicated by the position of the balance and the notions of 'heavier than' and 'lighter than' are refined. Spring scales for measuring weight can be used as the concept develops.

For linear measuring, where a pupil has difficulties with fine motor co-ordination, a ruler with a small handle can be used.

'Constructional' difficulties

A pupil having 'constructional' difficulties will tend to have problems understanding geometry and with understanding clocks and calendars. The 'construction' refers to being able to understand certain aspects of mathematics. Clearly, geometry involves an understanding of how shapes are constructed. Perhaps less obviously, at one level, understanding an analogue clock requires understanding of how the clock face is made up and of the relationships such as 'quarter to' 'quarter past' and so on. Similarly, reading calendars requires an understanding of how the grid and numbers are constructed.

A basic understanding of shapes can be developed through handling physical shapes, drawing around shape stencils, tracing shape outlines and similar activities. The names of the shapes can be regularly reinforced as such activities are taking place.

Mathematics and dyslexia

Dyslexia and mathematics difficulties

It has been stated that 'It would be remarkable if many of the children who have difficulty with literacy skills did not also have trouble with mathematics' (Pollock et al., 2004, p. 137). A consideration of some of the difficulties associated with dyslexia was made earlier in Chapter 2. These were: phonological difficulties; information processing difficulties; memory difficulties; co-ordination difficulties; organisational difficulties; sequencing difficulties; orientation difficulties; visual difficulties; and auditory processing difficulties. Each of these is considered below in relation to problems with mathematics for the pupil with dyslexia. Phonological and auditory difficulties are considered together at the outset (but other difficulties are dealt with in the same sequence as the chapters on dyslexia).

Phonological and auditory processing difficulties

Difficulties with phonological representations and with auditory processing and auditory perception may make it hard for the pupil with dyslexia to develop a secure understanding of the language of mathematics.

The pupil may have difficulty in acquiring and using mathematical language such as 'addition', 'place value', 'decimals' and 'fractions'. He may have limited experience of mathematical language, both in hearing it used and in using it himself. Using mathematical language correctly goes hand in hand with developing the understanding and skills with which the language is associated.

For pupils having difficulties with the language of mathematics, the teacher can encourage an interest in mathematics vocabulary for all pupils. New words will be introduced and explained and key words will be displayed throughout the lesson, for example on a board. Wall displays with key words as their focus can be built up as the new words have been introduced. The etymology of mathematics words is interesting and can help make the meaning clearer. For example, when the word 'triangle' is used, the teacher can draw attention to the 'tri' part of the word meaning 'three' and compare this with other examples of its use in words such as 'tricycle' and 'trident'.

The use of number stories aims to give the pupil a better understanding of word problems and how they are constructed (Poustie, 2001b, pp. 33–4). These might, for example, involve the pupil making up and telling a story about '3' and '7' – perhaps that there were seven children and three of them went out for a walk and that four were left. The pupil would then be encouraged to write the different sums that can be made from the story such as '7 − 3 = 4'.

Potentially misleading language may require careful explanations and examples. The fact that the numbers in, for example, 'twenty-three' are said with the 'tens' part of the number first but that a number such as 'fourteen' is said with the units part of the number first can be confusing to some children. A careful explanation with examples of the expression 'teen' meaning 'ten' and the rule that, for numbers 13 to 19, the number is said in this way will help deal with this anomaly.

Visual difficulties and visual processing difficulties

If there are visual difficulties, numerals and signs in mathematics may appear to the learner distorted or merged into each other, creating difficulties with accuracy. Numerals may be reversed so that, for example, 2 may be written as 5 and 45 may be written as 54. Multi-sensory teaching and learning, especially kinaesthetic-tactile activities, can help the pupil learn and internalise shapes of numerals more securely. The teacher can begin by introducing numerals with clear visual differences in shape such as 1 and 8, gradually teaching and testing the pupil's ability to discriminate the numerals that are nearer in shape such as 3 and 8. It is possible that confusion with numerals including reversals may be (depending on the child's age) part of the range of normal development, just as the reversal of alphabetical letters can occur with children who do not have difficulties with writing nor go on to have such difficulties with writing. But professional judgement has to be used where such features are marked or persistent as timely intervention will be necessary.

If there are visual processing difficulties, these may lead to difficulties scanning across lines of columns of numbers and keeping one's place with obvious implications for accuracy. Again squared paper can help.

Motor co-ordination difficulties

To the extent that a pupil with dyslexia has co-ordination difficulties, he may have problems with the fine motor movements necessary to legibly form numerals and mathematical symbols with potential implications for accuracy. Mistakes are easily made in setting out numerals and symbols in columns for calculations if the numbers are not aligned correctly. Using squared paper can help this. The pupil may have difficulty reproducing geometrical shapes and the teacher can give help and support for this by providing stencils, encouraging the pupil to track round the lines of printed shapes, and copying from a shape stencil beside him.

Difficulty with short-term verbal memory

Difficulties with short-term verbal memory may be apparent, perhaps in the pupil having difficulty remembering numbers. The pupil may have problems remembering multiplication tables or remembering the sequences of a mathematical operation.

A pupil's difficulties remembering numbers can be helped by the teacher having the pupil use concrete items with, if necessary, one-to-one tuition to help the pupil eventually retain the numbers mentally. The pupil may be helped to remember multiplication tables by approaches such as table grids using visual patterns such as having some numbers coloured (Poustie, 2001b, pp. 60–1). These allow the use of the visual sense as the pupil scrutinises the grid and the auditory mode as he hears himself or another person say the numbers.

If difficulties with short-term memory include problems remembering instructions and sequences of numbers, this has clear implications for mathematics learning. Multi-sensory teaching and learning will aid remembering information as will regular practice and over-learning, though not to the point of boredom. Part of multi-sensory learning is allowing the pupil to talk through the calculation. Mnemonics can help all pupils and well-known ones in mathematics include SOHCAHTOA to help remember the relationships for sine (opposite over hypotenuse); cosine (adjacent over hypotenuse) and tangent (opposite over adjacent).

In mental mathematics, the pupil with dyslexia may have difficulty retaining the information and at the same time processing it to calculate the solution. One strategy is for the teacher to allow the pupil to make only part of the task mental, writing down the key number and the sign for the mathematical operation. So, for example, if the problem is 8×9, the pupil will write down $8 \times$ and remember the 9 mentally and then work out the calculation mentally.

Physical aids to memory such as number lines and multiplication table squares can assist calculations. Visualising may help the pupil deal with otherwise abstract problems. The calculation $9 + 7 = 16$ would be visualised as 'I have nine books and I get another seven books making sixteen books altogether.' Some symbols can be remembered better with a visual clue. For example, the signs $<$ and $>$ can be easily confused so that a pupil may not remember if '$8 < a$' means 'a' is smaller than 8 or 'a' is greater than 8. If the signs are remembered as crocodile teeth with the mouth open more widely for the bigger number, it is easier to remember that '$8 < a$' means 8 is smaller than 'a'.

Sequencing difficulties

Effective planning often rests on the pupil knowing the sequence in which the tasks need to be done, an area a pupil with dyscalculia tends to find difficult. So careful explanations are particularly important with step-by-step guidance. The use of Mind Maps™, which allow information including sequences to be presented visually, may help the pupil who has difficulties in planning and organisation.

Normally calculations for ×, − and + involve working from right to left as in the calculation below, where one begins on the right adding the 5 units and the 3 units then moves to the left to add the 1 ten and the 8 tens.

$$15 +$$
$$83$$
$$\overline{98}$$

But when dividing one works from left to right as in the calculation below, in which one first divides the 8 tens by 2 then moves to the right to divide the 4 units by 2:

$$2\overline{)\,8\,4} \div$$

To the extent that a pupil with dyslexia has difficulties with sequencing, such procedures need to be explicitly taught and practised.

Sequences of numbers 1, 2, 3, 4 and so on will be taught perhaps in small steps so that the pupil will first learn the sequence 1, 2 securely then 1, 2, 3 and so on over several sessions as necessary.

Time sequences, such as the days of the week and the months of the year, can similarly be explicitly taught and practised using multi-sensory aids such as pictures or photographs associated with different days. Again the sequence can be learned in small steps. An example of teaching the sequence of numbers on a clock face (which also relates to constructional difficulties) was provided earlier in Chapter 3.

THINKING POINTS

Readers may wish to consider the extent to which in a particular school:

◆ approaches relating in general to dyscalculia are understood and used;
◆ approaches relating to dyspraxia and mathematical difficulties are understood and used;
◆ approaches relating to dyslexia and mathematical difficulties are understood and used;
◆ these can be rationalised into a comprehensive and coherent set of interventions.

KEY TEXTS

Butterworth, B. and Yeo, D. (2004) *Dyscalculia Guidance*, Windsor, NFER-Nelson.

This manual for teachers defines and describes dyscalculia and suggests classroom guidelines, teaching strategies and activities aimed at improving progress in mathematics.

_____

Henderson, A. (1998) *Maths for the Dyslexic: A Practical Guide*, London, David Fulton Publishers.

To the extent that the reader considers, with regard to a particular pupil, that difficulties with mathematics overlap with dyslexia, he or she will find this book useful in giving guidance on teaching strategies relating to number (chapter 6), algebra (chapter 7), shape, space and measure (chapter 8) and handling data (chapter 9).

_____

Poustie, J. (2001a) *Mathematics Solutions: An Introduction to Dyscalculia Part A – How to Identify, Assess and Manage Specific Learning Difficulties in Mathematics*, Taunton, Next Generation.

This booklet describes how different conditions considered to be found within the 'specific learning difficulty profile' affect how mathematics understanding and skill is acquired and used. It outlines practical strategies and gives information on various resources.

_____

Poustie, J. (2001b) *Mathematics Solutions: An Introduction to Dyscalculia Part B – How to Teach Children and Adults who have Specific Learning Difficulties in Mathematics*, Taunton, Next Generation

This booklet covers prerequisite skills for mathematics, teaching tips and resources. Particularly useful are the practical strategies for helping pupils with dyscalculia, such as the nine square multiplication tables grid (pp. 60–1), and guidance on the teaching of fractions using Cuisenaire rod 'grids'. The resources section is wide-ranging.

_____

Chapter 6

Conclusion

When considering specific learning difficulties broadly as SEN, a helpful starting point is the *Special Educational Needs Code of Practice* (DfES, 2001a), the guidance, *Data Collection by Type of Special Educational Needs* (DfES, 2003) and a consideration of the implications of the Education Act 1996.

With regard to dyslexia, characteristics of literacy difficulties concern reading, writing and spelling. Associated difficulties are considered to be: phonological difficulties, auditory perception and auditory processing difficulties, visual difficulties and visual processing difficulties, motor co-ordination difficulties, difficulties with short-term verbal memory, and sequencing problems.

Turning to dyspraxia, among its characteristics are difficulties with handwriting, physical activities including physical education and the motor organisational aspects of personal and social skills. Underpinning processes were considered to be gross and fine motor co-ordination (sensory, proprioceptive and vestibular) and perceptual-motor development (eye–hand co-ordination, visual form consistency, spatial position and spatial relationships).

With reference to dyscalculia, characteristics include problems with mathematical concepts and operations. Prerequisite skills were important. Some associated difficulties were considered to be general and some tended to relate to aspects of dyslexia and to dyspraxia.

Several features about the field of specific learning difficulties may well have struck the reader.

Estimates of the prevalence of dyslexia and dyspraxia are varied, and it is perhaps becoming rather a tired point to keep on saying that this reflects the different training, experience and background of those who assess. It is puzzling for parents (and others) to discover that their child 'has' dyslexia or dyspraxia or dyscalculia in one assessment setting and not in another, even allowing for variability in a child's performance at different times.

Similarly, when different specific learning difficulties are statutorily assessed, the criteria from LEA to LEA still vary, so that a parent can move from one LEA to another and find that his or her child had SEN in one place but not in another or vice versa. It is therefore encouraging that an increasing number of LEA officers are agreeing criteria for specific learning difficulties with local parents, schools and others. As such developments continue, we might be moving towards a position where, locally at least, people can agree what dyslexia or dyspraxia might be and when it is considered to exist, surely a modest aspiration.

The possible causal factors relating to specific learning difficulties are still being debated although evidence that certain factors are implicated is regarded as relatively convincing. For example, many consider the notion of a phonological deficit as an underlying basis for dyslexia to be plausible.

The associated difficulties of specific learning difficulties are sometimes similar and overlap, leading to both further difficulties in assessing and identifying particular conditions and the perception (or the reality) that the conditions often occur together. Research into possible neurological factors that may underpin some of these interrelationships is becoming increasingly relevant as imaging methods suitable to be used with children are being refined.

Political debates about what the expansion of specific learning difficulties reflects are perhaps a sign of the confusion surrounding estimates of prevalence, causation and associated difficulty/co-occurrence. It has been a long-held view by some that the expansion of non-normative 'conditions' may reflect the needs of professionals and middle-class parents rather than the needs of children (Tomlinson, 1982). The social class of parents who consider their child to have specific learning difficulties is not known, for example in appeals to the Special Educational Needs and Disability Tribunal (SENDIST). The longer this persists, the harder it is to dismiss concerns that the expansion is socially unfair and inequitable (see, for example, Farrell, 2004a, p. 29). On the other side of the debate are those who consider that there may be yet more people who are not identified and assessed as needing support.

LEAs, schools and others who are concerned to effectively educate pupils with specific learning difficulties have to steer through such potential confusions and debates. One way of doing this is to develop awareness of specific learning difficulties including what is known and what is not known and to develop a range of interventions that are being regularly evaluated.

An example of the complexities is provided by approaches to teaching and learning for pupils with dyscalculia. Literacy difficulties are central to dyslexia, and movement planning is a central difficulty in dyspraxia. Therefore, when mathematics difficulties are present, the emphasis of the difficulty may well be different and the implications for how the difficulty is approached may have different emphases. However, in the case of an individual pupil, interpretations of mathematics difficulties can be to some degree eclectic. Sometimes it is simply not clear why the particular problem arises and neither is it guaranteed that a particular approach is certain of success. The effective teacher will use whatever generalisations seem suitable concerning the extent to which the difficulties may be mainly dyslexic or dyspraxic in nature or whether they are not convincingly explained by either context. This will lead to a professionally informed approach where generalisations about dyslexia and dyspraxia are used as appropriate and regularly evaluated pragmatism informs approaches too.

The educator will consider any approaches or suggestions and ask such questions as:

1 What is the educational principle used? Repetition? Relating new information to a pupil's existing interests? Multi-sensory approaches to supposedly compensate for weaker mode or to play to a pupil's mode preference for learning?
2 Is the educational approach related to a difficulty associated with specific learning difficulties or is it simply good teaching practice (or both)?
3 Does the approach make sense in terms of what the specific learning difficulty is supposed to be?

As many teachers know, interventions such as those indicated in this book can often be seen to have an impact on the progress, attainment and self-esteem of pupils. A secure foundation is likely to be laid when teachers relate interventions to associated (and possibly underpinning) difficulties and directly to the main manifestations of the difficulty in a coherent way, recognising the interrelated nature of many associated difficulties and characteristics. This can form a basis for continuing to develop a coherent and effective pedagogy as the often foggy terrain of specific learning difficulties becomes clearer.

Addresses

Association of Educational Psychologists
26 The Avenue
Durham DH1 4ED

Tel: 0191 384 9512
Fax: 0191 386 5287
e-mail: aep@aep.org.uk
www.aep.org.uk

British Dyslexia Association
98 London Road
Reading
Berkshire RG1 5AU

Tel: 0118 966 8271
Fax: 0118 935 1927
e-mail: info@dyslexia.help-bda.demon.co.uk
www.bda-dyslexia.org.uk

> The umbrella organisation, which provides information on local organisations, courses for teachers, conferences, computer programs and literature.

The Chartered Society of Physiotherapy
14 Bedford Row
London WC1R 4ED

Tel: 020 7306 6666
Fax: 020 7306 6611
e-mail: csp@physio.org
www.csp.org.uk

College of Occupational Therapy
106–114 Borough High Street
London SE1 1LB

Tel: 020 7357 6480
Fax: 020 7450 2299
e-mail: www.cot.co.uk

Crick Software Ltd
Crick House
Boarden Close
Moulton Park
Northampton NN3 6LF

Tel: 01604 671 691
e-mail: info@cricksoft.com
www.cricksoft.com

Cuisenaire Company Ltd
PO Box 3391
Winnersh
Wokingham RG41 5DZ

Tel: 0118 978 9680
e-mail: admin@cuisenaire.co.uk
www.cuisenaire.co.uk

> Cuisenaire Rods provide a physical basis for learning the four rules of number, fractions, percentages and algebra.

Dyslexia Institute
Park House
Wick Road
Egham
Surrey TW20 0HH

Tel: 01784 222300
e-mail: info@dyslexia-inst.org.uk
www.dyslexia-inst.org.uk

The Dyspraxia Foundation
8 West Alley
Hitchin
Hertfordshire SG5 1EG

Tel (helpline): 01462 454 986 (Monday to Friday, 10 a.m.–2 p.m.)
Tel (administration): 01462 455 016
Fax: 01462 455 052
e-mail: dyspraxia@dyspraxiafoundation.org.uk
www.dyspraxiafoundation.org.uk

Fisher-Marriott Software
58 Victoria Road
Woodbridge
Suffolk IP12 1EL

Tel: 01394 387 050
e-mail: contact@fishermarriott.com
www.fishermarriott.com

Harcourt Assessment (The Psychological Corporation)
Halley Court
Jordan Hill
Oxford OX2 8EJ

Tel: 01865 888 188
Fax: 01865 314 348
e-mail: info@harcourt-uk.com
www.harcourt-uk.com

Helen Arkell Dyslexia Centre
Frencham
Farnham
Surrey GU10 3BW

Tel: 01252 792 400
e-mail: info@24dr.com
www.members.aol.com

IANSYST Ltd
The White House
72 Fen Road
Cambridge CB4 1UN

Tel: 01223 420 101
e-mail: sales@dyslexic.com
www.iansyst.co.uk

White Space Ltd
41 Mall Road
London W6 9DG

Tel/fax: 020 88748 5927

Publish the software *Numbershark*, suitable for learners aged 6 upwards (www.numbershark.co.uk). Intended to teach the four rules of number meaningfully. Includes games and activities for sorting, place value, pattern recognition, sorting coins and many other skills.

Wordshark offers computer games using sound, graphics and text to teach and consolidate word recognition and spelling.

Bibliography

Addy, L. M. (2004) *Speed Up! A Kinaesthetic Approach to Handwriting*, Cambridge, LDA Ltd.

American Psychiatric Association (2000) *Diagnostic and Statistical Manual of Mental Disorders IV – Text Revision* (4th edn), Washington DC, American Psychiatric Association.

Ayers, H. and Prytis, C. (2002) *An A to Z Practical Guide to Emotional and Behavioural Difficulties*, London, David Fulton Publishers.

Beaton, A. A. (2004) *Dyslexia, Reading and the Brain: A Sourcebook of Psychological and Biological Research*, London, Psychology Press.

Black, K. and Haskins, D. (1996) 'Including all children in TOP PLAY and BT TOP SPORT', *British Journal of Physical Education*, Primary PE Focus, Winter edn, 9: 11.

Blum, P. (2004) *Improving Low Reading Ages in the Secondary School*, London, RoutledgeFalmer.

Booth, T. and Ainscow, M. with Black-Hawkins, K. (2000) *Index for Inclusion*, Bristol, Centre for Studies in Inclusive Education.

British Psychological Society (1999) 'Dyslexia, literacy and psychological assessment', Report by a working party of the Division of Educational and Child Psychology of the British Psychological Society, Leicester, BPS.

Brooks, G. (2002) *What Works for Children with Literacy Difficulties? The Effectiveness of Intervention Schemes*, London, Department for Education and Science.

Bundy, A. (2002) 'Play in children with DCD: what we know and what we suspect', 5th Biennial Conference on Developmental Co-ordination Disorders, Banff, Alberta, Canada.

Butterworth, B. (2003) *Dyscalculia Screener*, Swindon, NFER-Nelson.

—— and Yeo, D. (2004) *Dyscalculia Guidance*, Windsor, NFER-Nelson.

Cermak, S. A., Gubbay, S. S. and Larkin, D. (2002) 'What is developmental co-ordination disorder?', in Cermak, S. A. and Larkin, D. (eds) *Developmental Co-ordination Disorder*, Albany, NY, Delmar, pp. 2–22.

Corkin, S. (1974) 'Serial order deficits in inferior readers', *Neuropsychologia* 12: 347–54.

Crawford, S. G., Wilson, B. N. and Dewey, D. (2001) 'Identifying developmental co-ordination disorder: consistency between tests', in *Children with Developmental Co-ordination Disorder: Strategies for Success*, Binghampton, NY, Hawthorne Press.

Crombie, M. and McColl, H. (2001) 'Dyslexia and the teaching of modern foreign languages', in Peer, L. and Reid, G. (eds) *Dyslexia: Successful Inclusion in the Secondary School*, London, David Fulton Publishers.

Dehaene, S., Dehaene-Lambertz, G. and Cohen, L. (1998) 'Abstract representations of numbers in the animal and human brain', *Trends in Neuroscience* 21 (8): 355–61.

——, Spelke, E., Pinel, P. *et al.* (1999) 'Sources of mathematical thinking: behaviour and brain imaging evidence', *Science* 284: 970–4.

Department for Education and Employment/Qualifications and Curriculum Authority (1999a) *The National Curriculum – Handbook for Primary Teachers in England: Key Stages 1 and 2*, London, DfEE/QCA.

—— (1999b) *The National Curriculum – Handbook for Secondary Teachers in England: Key Stages 3 and 4*, London, DfEE/QCA.

Department for Education and Skills (2001a) *Special Educational Needs Code of Practice*, London, DfES.

—— (2001b) *Inclusive Schooling: Children with Special Educational Needs*, London, DfES.

—— (2001c) *The National Numeracy Strategy Guidance to Support Pupils with Dyslexia and Dyscalculia*, London, DfES.

—— (2003) *Data Collection by Type of Special Educational Needs*, London, DfES.

Dixon, G. and Addy, L. M. (2004) *Making Inclusion Work for Children with Dyspraxia: Practical Strategies for Teachers*, London, RoutledgeFalmer.

Dykman, R. A. and Ackerman, P. T. (1992) 'Diagnosing dyslexia: IQ regression plus cut points', *Journal of Learning Disabilities* 25: 574–6.

El-Nagar, O. (1996) *Specific Learning Difficulties in Mathematics: A Classroom Approach*, Tamworth, National Association of Special Educational Needs.

Farrell, M. (2001) *Standards and Special Educational Needs*, London, Continuum.

—— (2003) *The Special Education Handbook*, London, David Fulton Publishers.

—— (2004a) *Special Educational Needs: A Resource for Practitioners*, London, Paul Chapman Publishing.

—— (2004b) *Inclusion at the Crossroads: Special Educational Needs – Concepts and Values*, London, David Fulton Publishers.

Fawcett, A. J. and Nicholson, R. I. (1992) 'Automatisation deficits in balance for dyslexic children', *Perceptual and Motor Skills* 75: 507–29.

—— and —— (2004a) *Dyslexia Screening Test – Junior*, London, Harcourt Assessment, Psychological Corporation.

—— and —— (2004b) *Dyslexia Screening Test – Secondary*, London, Harcourt Assessment, Psychological Corporation.

—— and —— and Dean, P. (1996) 'Impaired performance in children with dyslexia in a range of cerebellar tasks', *Annals of Dyslexia* 46.

Gartner, A. and Lipsky, D. K. (1989) 'New conceptualisations for special education', *European Journal of Special Needs Education* 4 (1): 16–21.

Gillberg, C. (1998) 'Hyperactivity, inattention and motor control problems: prevalence, comorbidity and background factors', *Folia Phoniatrica et Logopaedica* 50: 107–17.

Given, B. K. (1998) 'Psychological and neurobiological support for learning style instruction: why it works', *National Forum of Applied Educational Research Journal* 11 (1): 10–15.

Godfrey, J. J., Syrdal-Lasky, A. K., Millay, K. K. *et al.* (1981) 'Performance of dyslexic children on speech perception tests', *Journal of Experimental Child Psychology* 32: 401–24.

Goswami, U. (2004) 'Neuroscience, education and special education', *British Journal of Special Education* 31 (4): 175–83.

Greenwood, C. (2002) *Understanding the Needs of Parents: Guidelines for Effective Collaboration with Parents of Children with Special Educational Needs*, London, David Fulton Publishers.

Hagtvet, B. E. (1997) 'Phonological and linguistic-cognitive precursors of reading abilities', *Dyslexia* 3: 3.

Haslum, M. N. (1989) 'Predictors of dyslexia?', *Irish Journal of Psychology* 10: 622–30.

Hatcher, P. (2000) 'Sound links in reading and spelling with discrepancy defined dyslexics and children with moderate learning difficulties', *Reading and Writing: An Interdisciplinary Journal* 13: 257–72.

Henderson, A. (1998) *Maths for the Dyslexic: A Practical Guide*, London, David Fulton Publishers.

Henderson, S. and Sugden, D. (1992) *Movement ABC Battery for Children Manual*, London, Psychological Corporation.

Hornby, G. (2003) 'Counselling and guidance of parents', in Hornby, G., Hall, C. and Hall, E. *Counselling Pupils in Schools: Skills and Strategies for Teachers* (2nd edn), London, RoutledgeFalmer, pp. 129–40.

Horne, J. K., Singleton, C. H. and Thomas, K. V. (1999) *Lucid Assessment System for Schools (Secondary Version)*, Beverley, Lucid Creation Ltd.

Howell, J. and Dean, E. (1994) *Treating Phonological Disorders in Children: Metaphon – Theory to Practice*, London, Whurr.

Hulme, C. and Snowling, M. (1997) *Dyslexia: Biology, Cognition and Intervention*, London, Whurr.

——, Roodenreys, S., Schweikert, R. *et al.* (1997) 'Word frequency effects on short-term memory tasks: evidence for a reintegration process in immediate serial recall', *Journal of Experimental Psychology: Learning, Memory and Cognition* 23: 1217–32.

Irlen, H. L. (1994) 'Scotopic sensitivity: Irlen syndrome hypothesis and explanation of the syndrome', *Journal of Behavioural Optometry* 5: 65–6.

Kaplan, B., Dewy, D. M., Crawford, S. G. *et al.* (2001) 'The term comorbidity is of questionable value in reference to developmental disorders: data and theory', *Journal of Learning Disabilities* 34 (6) (November/December).

Keates, A. (2000) *Dyslexia and Information and Communications Technology: A Guide for Teachers and Parents*, London, David Fulton Publishers.

Kirby, A. and Drew, S. (2003) *Guide to Dyspraxia and Developmental Co-ordination Disorders*, London, David Fulton Publishers.

Kopera-Frye, K., Dahaene, S. and Streissguth, A. P. (1996) 'Impairments of number processing induced by prenatal alcohol exposure', *Neuropsychologia* 34: 1187–96.

Larkin, D. and Parker, H. E. (1999) 'Physical activity profiles of adolescents who have experienced motor learning difficulties', 11th International Symposium for Adapted Physical Activity, Quebec, Canada, IFAPA International Federation of Adapted Activities.

Lewis, A. (2004) 'And when did you last see your father? Exploring the views of children with learning difficulties/disabilities', *British Journal of Special Education* 31 (1): 3–9.

Lloyd, S. (1992) *The Phonics Handbook*, Chigwell, Jolly Learning.

McDougal, S. J., Hulme, C., Ellis, A. *et al.* (1994) 'Learning to read: the role of short-term memory and phonological skills', *Journal of Experimental Child Psychology* 58: 112–33.

Macintyre, C. and Deponio, P. (2003) *Identifying and Supporting Children with Specific Learning Difficulties: Looking Beyond the Label to Assess the Whole Child*, London, RoutledgeFalmer.

Martin, D. and Miller, C. (2003) *Speech and Language Difficulties in the Classroom*, London, David Fulton Publishers.

Menell, P., McAnally, K. I. and Stein, J. F. (1999) 'Psychophysical sensitivity and physiological response to amplitude modulation in adult dyslexic listeners', *Journal of Speech, Language and Hearing Research* 42: 797–803.

Miles, T. R. and Miles, E. (1990) *Dyslexia: A Hundred Years On*, Buckingham, Open University Press.

—— and —— (2004) *Dyslexia and Mathematics*, London, Routledge.

Olsen, J. Z. (2000) *Handwriting Without Tears™*, London, Harcourt Assessment.

Padsman, J. W., Rotteveel, J. J. and Maassen, B. (1998) 'Neurodevelopmental profile in low risk pre-term infants at five years of age', *European Journal of Paediatric Neurology* 2 (1): 7–17.

Palmer, S. (2000) 'Phonological recoding deficit in working memory of dyslexic teenagers', *Journal of Research in Reading* 23: 28–40.

Peer, L. (2001) 'Dyslexia and its manifestations in the secondary school', in Peer, L. and Reid, G. (eds) *Dyslexia: Successful Interventions in the Secondary School*, London, David Fulton Publishers.

—— and Reid, G. (2003) *Introduction to Dyslexia*, London, David Fulton Publishers.

Pennington, B. F. (1990) 'Annotation: the genetics of dyslexia', *Journal of Child Psychology and Psychiatry* 31: 193–201.

Pollock, J., Waller, E. and Politt, R. (2004) *Day-to-Day Dyslexia in the Classroom* (2nd edn), London, RoutledgeFalmer.

Portwood, M. (1999) *Identification and Intervention: Developmental Dyspraxia: A Practical Manual for Parents and Professionals* (2nd edn), London, David Fulton Publishers.

Poustie, J. (2001a) *Mathematics Solutions: An Introduction to Dyscalculia Part A – How to Identify, Assess and Manage Specific Learning Difficulties in Mathematics*, Taunton, Next Generation.

—— (2001b) *Mathematics Solutions: An Introduction to Dyscalculia Part B – How to Teach Children and Adults Who Have Specific Learning Difficulties in Mathematics*, Taunton, Next Generation.

Ramus, F. (2001) 'Talk of two theories', *Nature* 412: 393–5.

Richardson, A. J. and Ross, M. A. (2000) 'Fatty acid metabolism in neurodevelopmental disorder: a new perspective on associations between attention deficit/hyperactivity disorder, dyslexia, dyspraxia and the autistic spectrum', *Prostaglandins, Leukotrienes and Essential Fatty Acids* 63 (1/2): 1–9.

Riding, R. and Rayner, S. (1998) *Cognitive Styles and Learning Strategies: Understanding Style Differences in Learning and Behaviour*, London, David Fulton Publishers.

Senzer, B. (2001) *Dyscalculia: A Brief Overview* (www.rivermall.com/math/dycalcr.htm).

Share, D. L. (1995) 'Phonological recoding and self-teaching: *sine qua non* of reading acquisition', *Cognition* 55: 151–218.

Snowling, M. J. (2000) *Dyslexia*, Oxford, Blackwell.

Stanovich, K. (1994) 'Annotation: does dyslexia exist?', *Journal of Child Psychology and Psychiatry* 35 (4): 579–95.

Stein, J. F. (1995) 'A visual defect in dyslexia?', in Nicholson, R. I. and Fawcett, A. J. (eds) *Dyslexia in Children: Multidisciplinary Perspectives*, Hemel Hempstead, Harvester Wheatsheaf.

——, Talcott, J. and Witton, C. (2001) 'Dyslexia: the role of the magnocellular system', Paper presented at the 5th British Dyslexia Association Conference.

Task Force on Dyslexia (2001) *Report of the Dublin Government* (www.irlgov.ie/educ/pub.htm).

Tod, J. (2000) *Dyslexia: Individual Education Plans*, London, David Fulton Publishers.

Tomlinson, S. (1982) *A Sociology of Special Education*, London, Routledge & Kegan Paul.

Wade, J. (1999) 'Including all learners: QCA's approach', *British Journal of Special Education* 26 (2): 80–2.

Weedon, C. and Reid, G. (2003) *Special Needs Assessment Portfolio*, London, Hodder & Stoughton

Westwood, P. (2000) *Numeracy and Learning Difficulties: Approaches to Teaching and Assessment*, London, David Fulton Publishers.

Whittles, S. (1998) *Can You Hear Us?: Including the Views of Disabled Children and Young People*, London, Save the Children.

Wilkins, A. J. (1995) *Visual Stress*, Oxford, Oxford University Press.

Wolf, M. and O'Brien, B. (2001) 'On issues of time, fluency and intervention', in Fawcett, A. (ed.) *Dyslexia: Theory and Good Practice*, London, Whurr.

Zago, L., Pesenti, M., Mellet, E. *et al.* (2001) 'Neural correlates of simple and complex mental calculation', *Neuroimage* 13: 314–27.

Index